Shorts

of related interest

Pretending to be Normal
Living with Asperger's Syndrome (Autism Spectrum Disorder)
Expanded Edition
Liane Holliday Willey
Foreword by Tony Attwood
ISBN 978 1 84905 755 4
eISBN 978 0 85700 987 6

Nerdy, Shy, and Socially Inappropriate
A User Guide to an Asperger Life
Cynthia Kim
ISBN 978 1 84905 757 8
eISBN 978 0 85700 949 4

Shorts

Stories about Alcohol, Asperger Syndrome, and God

Tessie Regan

Jessica Kingsley *Publishers*
London and Philadelphia

This edition published in 2015
by Jessica Kingsley Publishers
73 Collier Street
London N1 9BE, UK
and
400 Market Street, Suite 400
Philadelphia, PA 19106, USA

www.jkp.com

First edition published by Tessie Regan in 2013

Library of Congress Cataloging in Publication Data
A CIP catalog record for this book is available from the Library of Congress

British Library Cataloguing in Publication Data
A CIP catalogue record for this book is available from the British Library

ISBN 978 1 84905 761 5
eISBN 978 0 85700 951 7

Printed and bound in Great Britain

Dedicated to Joshua and Caleb

CONTENTS

About this Book

I love to write and recently (as in the past five-ish years) love to read. However, in both cases I find that after about a page or so I am so distracted that I can't finish a sentence. That's when I became satisfied with writing shorter pieces. Pieces that could be read in ten minutes or less. That could be written on a napkin, a receipt or in worst case scenarios, on a real piece of paper. I gave up pretending to read 800-page novels because I was really just impressing myself by holding them. I stopped thinking about writing a novel with one plot and became relieved to know that I could write a "novel" of short pieces with about 100 plots or 150 if you read it drunk. It was a prayer answered for the lovely combination of having a short attention span and a lot of stories to tell. Stories about addiction, God, and being slightly south of sane. All of these pieces were written somewhere between 2001 and 2013. Some names have been changed because I don't want to be sued and because I respect their privacy.

Ass Burgers

The first time I heard the term I was sitting in the office of a very wise and patient psychologist. She also had red hair so I thought there was a strong probability that she might be Irish, and naturally I thought we might be dear friends in the real world. Except for the minor detail that I was institutionalized in her institution and I was a bat-shit crazy alcoholic. But besides that, we would probably be friends. Except I later found out she doesn't drink and then I thought we might be very bored in the real world.

"Have you ever heard of Asperger Syndrome?" she asked casually. I had never heard of this except that it was "trending" and would maybe be fashionable like ADHD in a decade or so. Before I answered I turned the word over in my head: "Aspergers." In the very creative and picture-filled world between my ears I saw the word as it sounded: Ass-Burgers. Then I pictured an industrial factory line bringing hamburger patties down a conveyor belt and at just the right moment a

large ass clad in a sterile white apron would sit on the burger.
Ass Burger. This made me grin and I forgot to answer.

"What?" she asks grinning because *obviously* something
very funny has happened.

"Nothing, just thinking. No, I don't know about
Aspergers."

I would slowly gather information and was largely
unimpressed by the diagnosis. I know that historically people
stop and ponder the finer things of life when receiving a
diagnosis. It wasn't like I was going to die. It wasn't spreading
and eating my flesh. I had very little to be upset about. This
seemed much less like a diagnosis and much more like an
explanation. Peculiar and difficult blocks of my life started to
fall into place with more grace and more understanding. A
collective sigh of relief plumed from my sisters and friends.
I felt vindicated…it was real. I wasn't completely out of my
mind. The ugly and fruitless cycle of "Was her head screwy
and that led to drinking?" or "Did drinking make her head
screwy?" seemed to finally be pushed aside as a pointless
debate. It no longer mattered if it was the chicken or the
egg; it was quite simply a nest from which both beautiful and
damaged things came.

The first time I acknowledged to myself that something
was different with my mind was when I was in the sixth grade.
I was in class staring at the word "Apostrophe" written on the
chalkboard. The word seemed too big and elegant to represent
such a tiny little slip of the pen. The letters didn't look right
and the fact that it was capitalized was disconcerting to me.
The capital letter threw me off so significantly that I did not
know what the word was until I later asked the teacher after
class what the "A" word was on the board. But during this

class, as I was deep in thought over this word, I was suddenly struck with a direct and frank conversation. I said to myself that something was wrong with my head and that it was okay and no one should panic and that it would be okay eventually.

Eventually turned out to be a very precise date when I was 13 and I found alcohol. The bitter magic seemed to grease the squeaky and rusty cogs and wheels in my head. Things ran smoothly. Things got quieter. Things in the world seemed more approachable and real. Less like the fragile, sensory-imploding world that went unchallenged when dry and sober. At the time, it didn't even seem like I was choosing between one lesser evil over another. The mind seemed disconnected at the stem of my spine and whirled on and on to its own rhythm, I was just a random human attached to the other end of the stem. The beer rose to action and did what I could not and did what others could not because I could not figure out how to describe what was hurting. Looking back, I see that with the limited logic and articulation of a teenager, I had only one option. And that was to wait until I could explain the devils that came with me and the ones I invited in. As years would pass and the drinking and drugging became center stage, all other human parts of me would become obscured and hidden.

This great packing up would include the hiding away of all the things that drove me mad with anger and self-loathing. Why did my mind do these things? Why does this drinking betray me like this? I had energy for one thing and that was addiction. Then you find yourself on the outskirts of Amish country in the cold hills of Pennsylvania and people begin to probe and measure and count the ways in which you are still human. Those people begin to breathe life back into the dead things like a resurrection of zombies because some of them we'd wish would have stayed dead. First they fed me. Then gave me warm water and clean towels. Then I followed people around who did normal people things and I mimicked their normal people ways. And right about the time my organs began to deflate and fall back into their assigned locations my mind perked up with renewed vigor and love of blood that is rich with caffeine and nicotine, but, praise God, no alcohol.

Let me save you a trip to Google. Aspergers is a neurological issue, although I won't be offended if you just call it a mental illness. Like autism, it presents on a spectrum and will look and feel different for everyone. I was told about Aspergers relatively late in life, and I'm grateful for that. A hallmark for Aspergers is a social weirdness that is hard to tolerate. As a child and teen and young adult I was in survival mode and had profoundly good people to copy. Out of necessity, I *learned* how things were done. I'm told that most people don't learn about being human, that it just comes instinctively, and perhaps this is why when I try to describe it to people they leave the conversation thinking that I am absolutely mentally ill.

I think if I had known as a child what was misfiring I would not have become self-reliant and clever and resourceful. Now granted, one of my clever discoveries was alcohol and cocaine, but nonetheless, I made it. The drinking washed away the "steel-wool in my temples" feeling. The square blocks in my sternum. The clenching jaw that kept in screaming out loud because my skin was electric. Sometimes it is like being dropped off by the mother ship to run some experiments on the earthlings, but they forgot to give me the bone and flesh suit that can withstand the elements. Like sending a football player into the game without pads and a helmet. Oops.

As a baby I was colicky and difficult, but I'm pretty sure I was still cute as hell in that "Isn't it cute when it sleeps?" sort of way. As a child I was quiet, private, turned inward in a way that led to tantrums, and from the perspective of the other people in the room, probably frustrating. As a teenager I became angry and more private and wanted to be alone while at the same time wanting company, but on my own terms. I came across as selfish in many ways and an old soul in many ways too. My skin crawled for years and the pain and itch of not knowing what to do created anxiety and depression. It created a sensitivity and short-temperedness that was hard to predict and harder to soothe.

As an adult with more answers and more words, I feel profoundly sorry for my family who lived with this. The best answer we had was that I was quirky or bored or had a short attention span. And all of those answers were true! They just did very little to settle the matter. Also as an adult I can say that the way my mind works isn't all that bad because now I have the blessing of time having passed. But if it were my child revolting against some unseen world, I would be devastated. This is how time works. It makes us old and wise and forgetful and forgiving of the children we were. Of the things we ignored. Of the people we wounded.

On the other hand, this is why the Ass Burgers don't feel like a doom and gloom shitty hand of cards. I experience the world differently and it is wild for the most part. I have five senses that work on overdrive and filter the world much faster and much more precisely than they should. I notice everything in texture and color and scent and tone. The world is so alive pulsing through my body that it seems to have more personality than most of us. Sometimes two senses will mix and I feel what I'm seeing or I can hear what I'm feeling.

I am driven to gather this sensory information a lot of times without realizing I am doing it. Case in point: I used to work at an old folks' home and one night I was under the table vacuuming after dinner. I found a small, marble-sized green ball. Without thinking or pausing I put the ball in my mouth and bit it. Turns out it was a paint ball with neon orange paint inside. I stand up from under the table with orange paint drooling out of my mouth like blood. How am I supposed to explain this? I know how ridiculous the explanation would be! I know how hilarious I look! But in the moment, it wasn't enough to just feel the ball. I had to figure out what it was, so I put it in my mouth. Duh.

I am captivated by sounds, vibrations, and movements. There is a large fan in the ceiling of my church and sometimes I find that I have missed large chunks of the service because I've been reveling in watching the fan. My taste buds are spectacularly sensitive and have preferred the same seven to ten foods for my entire life. The things I ate as a child, I still eat exclusively as an adult. No spices, no sweets, no condiments, not much meat because of the texture. I would wear the same three pieces of clothing all the time because I like how they feel, but this would be weird to other people and so I refrain from my dangerous ways. Sometimes I think that alcohol and I were such fast friends because I responded to it with my *whole* body. Everything reacted at once and I think this probably flattered the alcohol. "All for me? Why how nice to be so thoroughly appreciated!" he would say. Most people drink and only one or two of their senses respond to it. You thought that buzz was nice? You should try it with 85 senses firing at once. Bam, I win again.

Another magical piece. Things never really stop. Words and lines and images live on and on in a digitally re-mastered extravaganza. Words lead to more words that are synonyms or translated to Spanish or to sign language or to a long line of ornate Pictionary symbols. Those same words are pulled up from past places the same words appeared. The last time I heard the word. The way the word looks typed versus written versus cursive. The way the word has duel meaning either by way of homophones or just by the cruelty of the English language. This recycling goes on ad nauseam until something more interesting interrupts it. Something like a street sign and I wonder what company makes these because I have passed 15 already and that seems like a lucrative endeavor. Or the sound of the coffee pot breathing.

I am a lover of consistency and routine. Any minor change results in anxiety and wanting to be alone. Anything from my older sister moving out of the country to the corner grocery store changing the layout of the aisles. Speaking of grocery stores, I hate them, I hate most stores in general because of the amount of options and the fluorescent lights. Marketing companies love people like me because I most often buy the item on display at the end of the aisle rather than go down the aisle and look at all the options. Unlike most people, I prefer one to three options at most. And this goes for everything. When I am asked what I want for dinner, I either ask for what I had the night before or I stall long enough for an idea to be given to me. It is as though every option known to man is racing by on a ticker tape in my mind and I'm supposed to choose one. I normally resort to just "picking" what I chose the last time.

I forget to do regular people things unless I see someone else do them. For example, brushing my teeth, changing my sheets, buckling my seatbelt, eating meals, taking medicine, and so on. These nuances in particular make me an easy target for being called lazy or absent-minded, but in reality they just do not occur to me. What in God's name is going on in your head that you could forget to eat!? Well, a lot. A lot of naming and listing and weird word games. A lot of association and virtual writing. For example, I was trying to open a bag of cheese the other day and while trying to pry it open I was thinking about all the types of cheeses that I like and the names of cheeses that could also be proper nouns. I was so consumed by this task that I didn't realize I was opening it at the wrong end. Didn't realize it until I cut open the bottom and laid it on the counter only to see the re-sealable zipper on the top. Or another prime example happened when I was shaving my legs recently. I noticed that my socks had left an indention in my skin about half way up my calf. I became so focused on the indention and it sort of became a "line" and without thinking I started shaving at the "line." A couple days later I showed my sister my "hair sock" that resulted from only shaving the upper half of my legs.

There is a lot of time alone because I enjoy solitude and also because I need to "reset." There is a lot of avoiding and making lame excuses because I don't want to do something and this hurts people's feelings. They make wide circles and annoyed groans. They roll their eyes and suspect I didn't see it because I don't look them in the eye anyway. They wonder when I'll grow up or mature or act my age. And sometimes, they earnestly believe this is because I drank for so many years. That I gave myself some sort of permanent brain damage. But the misunderstanding is okay. When sunlight picks up the hairs on my bare skin one at a time and raises the temperature degree by miniscule degree, when I can watch and see this miracle happening on my arm, I will remember that some people will not even notice the warmth of it at all.

I will remember that my bag of tricks is a blessing translated for the earthlings as "quirky" and let it be well to be that too. It can be exhausting and it can be hilarious—and that is the best way I have of describing it.

Restoration of Sanity

Restoration: to put back to original form and function.

Sanity: of sound mind and spirit.

I've always heard that crazy people don't realize they are crazy. And that non-crazy people are such because they are aware of their neuroses. I find this hard to believe across the board. I've been most insane while drunk or high and even in these extreme states I've always known that my mind was slipping away and having less and less say-so in the matter of life. I was crazy and knew I was crazy. So I'm not sure which category that lands me in. Sometimes I think that there are very few, if any, people operating out of a "sane" mind. I think mostly we are way off kilter and occasionally experience sanity. But because humans don't fare well with broken things, we just lower the "sane" bar and pretend we all made the cut, when in reality the standards just qualified a chimpanzee as rational. I don't really have a bad taste about insanity or craziness. I'm not sure it would actually be possible to live and breathe in the world as the levelheaded, well-adjusted, competent people we make others believe we are. I think my indifference to depravity of mind has allowed me to be more creative in adjusting to it. I'm not saying I embrace and applaud the insanity of my addiction, I'm just saying that the maladjusted brain I was born with was ill-equipped from womb to womanhood and alcohol simply made the symptoms move from "something is off" to "bat-shit crazy." My sober crazy is a lot easier for other people to tolerate. My drunk crazy made other people back away slowly. I don't like the drunk crazy either, but I really dislike the sober crazy.

When I was drunk or high I turned into something that I never fully recognized. My mind was quiet and this was the reward. For about 17 years that reward of silence out-weighed every dreadful consequence. Everything that was good and right and justifiably mine was gone. It was all gone and yet I continued to pursue dying because the reward was still sweet for a splitting second. It is agony to have sacrificed everything for something that has betrayed me in the end. And then just as quickly as my soul bottomed out, I found myself sobering up in a detox. In terms of restoration, my body and organs would slowly return to relative health. My appetite and sleep would improve. My medicine would begin to work as it was intended to. But my mind would go back to the "sober crazy." It's not actually "insanity" but the misgivings of my mind have led me to a number of unravelings, even while stone cold sober. My head hurts, but this is the default setting, the base line and this often feels like an unfair gift. When I think about God restoring my mind, I struggle to imagine what it is He would choose. My drunk head was no good because it invited death the way coffee lulls me out of bed. But my sober head, although much healthier, resists in so many ways. I don't want to be restored to this sober head.

I don't want to believe that God would want a restoration to have so many loopholes. What I know I'm supposed to say and believe is that God will make a restoration by healing and providing ways, both of which will be novel and life giving. But in my gut I know that my head will continue to misfire and I should begin praying for direction in untangling the loopholes.

The more hours I am sober, the more I am aware of why I stayed inebriated. It is harsh and tricky and full of things that make me question the decision to remain dry. I think about dying a lot. I think about leaving home. I think about staying dry for the rest of my life. I think about how the world feels soft and steely at the same time and then not at all. How the inseam of my jeans makes a good case to drink because it bothers my leg. How when the cadence of the prayer changes from the way we do it in the South I imagine smacking their faces. Then I think about how I cried and how salty it was in my mouth and warm it made my eyes, and how it felt incredibly human to cry. How it feels human and dare I say normal, to eat three times a day. To have a clean bed. How it feels to remember small things. I think about laughing hard and making people laugh. I think about the soft, steely earth and how unforgiving and merciful she seems to be at the same time and then not at all. I feel like a fish who understands the world because it takes the world through its body. The sober world is strange, but it has allowed me room enough to try.

FISH BREATHE BECAUSE AS WATER passes over their bodies, their gills open and pull oxygen from the water. I imagine that this is the way I experience the world. I live in an entirely palpable and vivid and chaotic world. My experience and processing of the world is entirely a physical one. Not an emotional or spiritual one. The way water passes through a fish every few seconds, the world passes through my senses every few seconds, and it registers on so many levels that I begin to believe I've been given more than five senses. But I've learned and become adept at maneuvering. It is blatantly obvious that others do not feel the world the way I do, so I've figured out how to not react. How to mimic and match. How to manipulate the environment to make it less like water and more like air.

Tessie

Lawnmower

A friend of mine asked if I wanted to help her mother with some yard work in order to make a little extra money. I readily agreed and was given instructions to show up on a Saturday around 10am. That Saturday, at the prospect of making an easy $100, I showed up early with an eagerness that only broke people can muster.

When I turned down the long winding driveway it became obvious that this was perhaps the largest yard in the history of grass. It felt more like the last frontier or like there should have been a rest stop half way down the driveway. I meet the mother, and to this day I'm still not sure how to pronounce her name. She tells me I "just" need to mow the lawn and not to worry about the little stuff. And then she drags out an electric lawnmower that would have been more useful for shaving. I stand there looking at the mower between us and am really trying to suppress my laughter, but the thing is, she is dead serious. She actually wants me to use this micro-machine to mow most of North America. But like I said, broke people do stupid things to get a little cash. I've done worse in fact; a few times I mowed my drug dealer's yard to get a baggy. Then someone stole my lawnmower and that entrepreneurial spirit was snatched away.

I bring the mower and back-up battery out to the very front of the yard, like I'm going to start up here and make my way back toward the house maybe sometime next month. And the mother sat on the porch in her large straw sunhat with a cup of iced tea and watched me trek out to the front of the property line. "I'm going to mow that bitch over with this piece of shit," I think as I make my way. I start mowing and realize almost immediately that I'm going to have to run over an animal or something to break the mower and end the whole ordeal right here and now.

I get about 50 yards before the blades get bloated and clogged with grass. I kill both batteries after about 45 minutes. I am sweating profusely and I've mowed an area about the size of a suburban. I head back down to the mother and as politely as I can, I tell her that this mower wasn't made for this sort of job. She suggests that instead of the batteries I get the extension cords out. I think to myself that she would need about five miles of cord to get out there, but instead I say, "I don't think that will work either, it's just not made to do this." And then without any more debate she gives me $100, tells me to go home and rest and to come back tomorrow. I think maybe the heat has gone to her head or maybe it wasn't iced tea she was drinking. I take the money and go home and lay in front of the air conditioning vent for hours.

The next day I go back. I know, stupid, hopeless pursuit, but I went anyway. And when she opens the garage this time it is like a choir of angels appeared...a riding John Deere lawnmower. Brand new, shiny, powerful, gas-powered and with a seat. This machine was made to do this job. She asks if I know how to work it and although it is a lie I excitedly tell her that I absolutely do know how, for fear that if I say I don't know then she'll bring out the mini-clipper again. I actually don't know how to operate this thing at all, I don't even know how to get it started. But I get on it and she stands nervously to the side. I read over the operating manual in a hurry and jerk the thing to life. It lurches backward, and almost on a wheelie, I'm plowing in reverse out of the garage and into the yard. She is screaming and clapping with approval and praise and I ride the most amazing piece of machinery I've ever seen out into the yard that now looks so much less daunting.

Now it just looks like a yard and I hungrily eat it up without much straining or effort. It still takes about four hours but it looks wonderful and she waves at me from her perch every time I ride by. She flags me down at one point to make me wear sunscreen and to drink some water, but I don't dare turn it off in case I can't figure out how to get it started again. She pays me handsomely and praises my hard work. The truth, though, is that this didn't get done because she had a lot of money or because I'm a hard worker, it got done because I had a machine that was created to do the job at hand.

That's what God means when He says I was created to praise and know Him. I was created for a very specific purpose and when I do something other than that it becomes laborious and painful and worthless, even idiotic. Like mowing all those acres with a toaster on wheels.

Spiritual?

(This letter was written to a high school class of students in response to one of their questions they asked me while I was visiting their school.)

One of you asked about my "spiritual life story." I thought this was important enough not to blow off and I apologize for not being more articulate about it in your class. I'll admit, I know very little about God and Jesus and the bible and all that other holy-roller stuff. I know a little bit about faith and hope and love and kindness, but I know an awful lot about what lives on the other side of those things. And in all honesty, this is where my spirit died and was later redeemed – in the quiet shadows of despair. This is not the best way to go about "finding God" and I do not recommend it to anyone, but this is how it happened for me. Like if you wanted a new best friend, you wouldn't start by slapping people in the face.

I actually grew up going to an Episcopal church in West Virginia, but we weren't going because we were convicted by and changed by God's personality, we were going because it gave people a stage and we wanted to watch what happened when regular people pretended to be more than that little coal town allowed them to be. And because the church had food. Lame reasons, but reasons nonetheless. I never thought of God as personal and absolutely never cried out to Him. I was raised to do it myself, not to complain and to rely on my own ability to muddle through. Even if my way was messy and ugly and replete with glaring mistakes, at least I could say, "I did it again!" Terribly self-reliant, scared to death and constantly out of options.

Many years later, as a teenager, I began to develop my understanding of God by way of blaming Him for everything. My anger for God was real and palpable and I let it swell into a thing that didn't have anything to do with God at all. I was fighting myself and the wailing and worthlessness of this fight would not abate for many more years. I was losing my mind and I knew it and I could not cry out to God. To me, God was an ideal that idiots made up and was a sweet way for adults to continue to behave like children. It is sort of like asking middle-aged people to suddenly believe in Santa Claus, and the real shocker is that they willingly believe! They start making Christmas lists and leaving cookies out for this fat man and they hang socks on their mantels. They start behaving like Santa exists and from the sidelines they look completely insane. This is what "faith" looked like for me and it certainly didn't mean anything about redemption and healing and resolution.

When I met my best friends in college and they began talking about a god that was intimately connected to their lives and that this same god was aware of my life and longed to love me the same way, I was immediately appalled. I wanted none of this "loving god" who had just changed out of his Santa suit at the mall and was now sitting in the clouds dropping blessings down to do-gooders like a stork drops a baby. This all-knowing god who witnessed the horror of my life, this father-god who was to love me in this manner, this loving god who would forgive me of things I would not give voice to. This god was stupid for being a pushover and a fool. This god who would not let me die already. Who kept breath in my lungs. Who saw all the underlying pieces of my life as organized and ordered. This god would not fit into my world because he was very small and very incompetent.

When I was really drunk I would allow myself the luxury of pining for Christ. I would allow myself to feel pulled to His ideals and I would, for a couple of hours, acknowledge that this idea was very attractive. It made no sense, it did not make me feel better, it did not make me giddy with dumb-struck love, it did not wipe away the shit, it actually felt very idiotic to even give it a second glance. But when it all came to a head, I could not deny that I was over my head and I could not come up with an answer. I laid on the floor of the suicide cell in the county jail and I was completely aware of my inability to heal myself. Not only that, but I knew with deadly certainty that I would do myself no favors by pretending I knew how do make any good or right decisions.

I was, in effect, completely at the mercy of a faith that only surfaced in naked desperation and in semi-conscious drunkenness. But. This improbable and ridiculous notion was enough. I wouldn't even call it "blind faith," I would just call it "shit out of luck" and when I had to weep from my belly, from the part of me that I thought had died a decade ago – when that part of me wept with conviction, it wept for Christ. It wailed without dignity and without hope. People like to think of God swooping in and making a Cinderella story of assholes like myself. But the really uncomfortable truth is that when I was dying, when I was busted broke by the world, all I could do was cry and pray really simple prayers. I had no composure and no grand finale. I simply begged like the dog under the Thanksgiving table. Just throw me a scrap Jesus, just throw me the bone or the crumb and I will be satisfied.

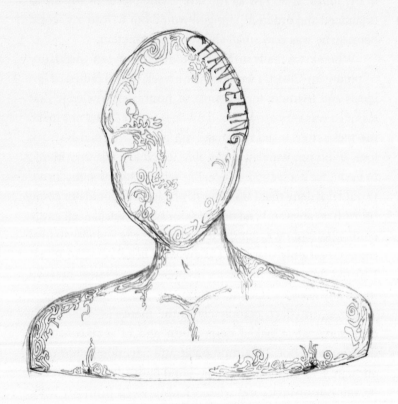

This is always the part where people want me to say, "Praise God, Alleluia, verse 10 through 20, amen sister mother of Mary." But what happened next is just what happens when a little human gets acquainted with a massive god. A god that I want my words to write circles around, but all they do is fall heavy on a page without any clarity. A god that I want a picture of, like if I could see his face then I would have a better sense of what I'm getting myself into. In reality I know this wouldn't actually happen. I have a shortsighted perspective and am clouded with judgment and hurt feelings. If I saw God's face I would probably crap my pants and then tell myself that He looks different than I imagined and this was probably a late-surfacing hallucination from the drugs.

Anyway, after I got out of jail I continued to drink and use narcotics for another three years. I was plagued by God's sadness over my indecision. I could feel a pressure building, like I knew I was on borrowed time, but I was too sick to pull the brakes. It felt too late and too far-gone to start over. A lot of people have told me in letters that they admire my "decision to change" or my "ability to turn my life around." I want to be perfectly clear about this. I did not change my life. I did not pull myself up by the bootstraps and suddenly muster the strength to live. I simply gave in completely. I was exhausted and thoroughly beaten. On the outside, I can see why it would look like I slowly started to rebuild my life. But believe me when I say, I was no more capable of rerouting my life than I was of buying groceries. I was hopeless and I did not have the capacity to change. I was given a very strange gift of desperation. When you are desperate for relief, really really hungry for the oppression to ease, then you stop acting at all, in all areas of your life, and this allows for God to start acting to a degree in all areas. So, although it sounds backwards, it is because I stopped trying that I started to have a chance at all.

Again, please do not think I orchestrated this recovery. I am no fool about this matter and I am very sure that God put this together, that He saved me from myself and that He put in motion the slowest evolution of a faith that ever existed.

I do not have anything figured out and I certainly still carry a load of resentments and frustrations about what it means for me to believe in God. I still get very angry and silenced by the hard questions that Jesus forces me to look at. I can't say that I think Jesus is so awesome and great that I just can't stand myself. I am extremely human and I think Jesus is a little bit ridiculous for pulling this "savior" stunt in the first place. I think He is incapable of healing me, I think He created a sad, sad world and I think I need Him more immediately than I will ever be able to recognize. I need mercy like that damn dog under the table, staring with hungry eyes at my plate.

Woodworking

Down in my basement I have a little workshop set up to make stuff. Mostly it's furniture that turns out, but a lot of times too it's just things that happened to get nailed together. The basement used to be tidy, smelled a little like water damage, and carried a lingering sense of something spooky living down there, the way any good basement can make anyone nervous simply because it is dark and damp and dim. My sister avoided it at all costs. She went down there to change the loads of laundry and then ran back up before she got swallowed up by the quiet, crouching thing that lives in the corner. In reality it's just a massive lint ball and a few spiders, but when you're down there by yourself you are willing to bet it is something wild from the book of Revelation. Something big enough to eat your soul while you fold the white load. Something quick enough to grab your ankles in between the creaking stairs while you run back up them.

But then I got this bright idea to make it into a workshop. My sister obviously didn't object; to her I was asking if she minded if I used a corner of hell to set up shop. I cleaned it up and organized the storage that had accumulated from multiple different people not fortunate enough to have their own scary basements to store things. Things that are not important enough to go upstairs but are too important to throw away. We have a lot of that kind of stuff and I hate it. Why don't I just throw away that shit? Why would I ever need to reference my high school yearbooks? Why do I need this memorabilia from a young girl who I feel sad for and miss and at the same time wish I never saw her face before so that I would never have to remember it in nostalgia? At any rate, my doomed basement turned into a storage center, save the fees and automated gate, for a bunch of folks. Had I been on top of my game I could have started charging people per square foot. Hindsight is a bitter bitch.

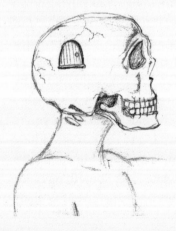 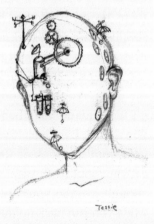

So the workshop was up and running and I would go down there with a cup of coffee and some music and start cutting twice and measuring once. And my sister would come down periodically to make sure I hadn't cut off a finger or passed out from the fumes of wood stain. And then she started coming down to check on the progress of my projects because she loved them and couldn't wait to get them upstairs. She stopped saying Hail Marys before descending the stairs to the basement because it started to be a part of the house rather than the terrible ghetto where the washer and dryer had to live.

The first thing I made was an end table and it was a marvel. Nothing fancy, just sturdy and square and well made. I sanded it with the care I imagine someone takes when icing a cake. It was smooth from my hand and it took the stain all the better. And it was heavy substantial, and deserved the spot in the room we put it. It would not knock over and it would not break. It was not fragile. and this is why I love making things with wood.

I have seen a lot of fragile things shatter hopelessly before me and after so many of these, you start to wish that things were made of steel and wood rather than flesh and bone. The wood in my basement is unforgiving and reduces my hands to blisters and scratches within a couple of hours. It does not care that my skin tears so easily and it does not care that the floor I carelessly drop it on is as hard. It just collides and smashes and leaves dents and scrapes in its wake. It is not fragile and it is not humble. When I misalign the screws or overfill a damp hole with putty, the wood does not blush and try to accommodate the error. It lays it out in obscene clarity. "Look at this mistake!" And then I go back to it and coddle it and fix it because it will not placate me, I must bow to its resilience and to my inclination to ruin it twice before getting it right. I love how opposed to fragility it is. Even a really little, thin piece of wood is not to be ignored. A splinter of wood in my finger is as irritating as its mother board plowing off the shelf and ruthlessly smashing into my foot. Or I forget the goggles, which is more often than not, and the sawdust finds my big green eyeballs like a moth to the flame. And you can't blink that shit out, you have to stop everything, go all the way upstairs (half blind), take out the contacts and rinse it all out. And then as you make your way back downstairs to the basement your sister casually asks if you were wearing your goggles down there.

While I was making the coffee table that is now in my living room, I used pre-treated 2×4s, so they were damp while I was working them. Or I guess I should say, while they were working me. I made the entire thing in a few hours, sanded and stained, it was clearly a world record. Three days after completion the treatment on the boards finally absorbed and dried and the boards shrank, leaving gaps in between my painstakingly laid boards. And the putty was pushed upward by the force of a board drying and tightening the air around the holes. I learned a few things with this project: (1) Never buy pre-treated wood again; (2) Because the wood wasn't ready, I turned it into something unintended. If I had waited for it to dry, or if I had at least known this would happen, then this project would have been a homerun. This one would have turned out flawless. But now I'm left with these irregular gaps and bumps and I stare at them periodically when I'm supposed to be looking at the television just beyond it. I stare at them and they mock me: "I will not adapt to your wishes. I will always do what wood wants." My sister says the gaps make it look "rustic" and "vintage." I sort of believe her because she watches HGTV religiously, but I also think she must be wondering if I even have a measuring tape downstairs.

And this is why I wish we were made of wood, because I could just do things the way that felt natural to me and I would not have to worry about tearing blisters through other people's expectations and assumptions. I would stop worrying about learning to make habits of "normal" adult things. The problem is not that I worry what others are thinking, in fact I don't really think I have the attention span for that. The problem is that I know I do things differently and this creates a strange world to live in. I want to care about myself, but I don't care enough to brush my teeth. I want to have no reaction when I undress for a shower, but I end up in the dark and staring straight ahead. I want to think that snuggling up in my bed at night will be restful and refreshing, but I know it will be riddled with things I should have thrown away with the unimportant boxes of storage.

I wish I had the balls to just go around living up to my natural elements the way wood does, but I live in a strange world and the wood gets to live in the basement. I am also well aware that living like this would mean a short life for me because my natural elements happen to be wired for death. But I think everyone is wired a little bit for natural self-destruction. Like if we are left alone for a little too long then we start to make decisions that resemble insanity, but they feel so sure in the moment.

I think everyone has this propensity, but most people abate it with social norms and stable families and realistic plans and other good things. I go around wishing I didn't have to take care of fragile things. Things like relationships, health, wellness, sobriety, and so on. These are unfair things. These things take so long to build up and sustain and then in a literal minute they are wiped from the buffet. In one split moment of time, the universe opens her greedy jaws and swallows what was mine. And I can try to pry them back from her. I can try to negotiate and grovel and sacrifice, but ultimately once she takes them then they are not the same even if I do get them back. The way a wounded friend smiles at you, years after the injustices took place. Her smile smells of an unforgetting wound, a wound that I caused, and smiling doesn't make it better. Apologizing doesn't make it better. Hanging out doesn't make it go back to normal because I can see that she really means to ask, "Why would you do those things?" But she can't say that because she's civilized and lives like a normal person made of flesh that bruises so easily.

Or the way that you feel when you realize your parents are actually people aside from "Mom" and "Dad." This shocking moment when you see your mother interacting with someone as a friend or sibling and you suddenly feel her motherliness slip away into some sweet dream where mothers were only allowed to be mothers. Before I knew this; I wish the universe would give that back to me.

Or the way hypothetical relationships and marriage evaporate in a plume of smoke. And no grade of sandpaper makes this better. There are not enough power saws in the world to chop and shuffle those pieces.

At the end of the day, I don't get to choose not to adapt like the wood or nails. I have to give in to this strange world, I have to negotiate and I have to make room for the pieces that I didn't intend and fill up the spots where pieces were taken. The strange world seems more and more likely to be the one that keeps the quiet, crouching thing in the corner.

Shrapnel

Last year (or maybe this happened ten years ago and I just don't know things) Satan needed a new way for people to waste whole chunks of their day, so he invented Pinterest. Who knew so much of the world really thought kittens were *that* cute and that nail polish was "postable" and necessary commentary. At any rate, Satan wins again and I have a permanent red mark on my stomach from where the laptop sat streaming Pinterest for days. In all of my diligence though, I did find something that set off a domino chain in my warped and cluttered mind. There was a letter from a kid written to God and it said, "Dear God, please put another holiday between Christmas and Easter because right now there is nothing good in there." Smart kid. I thought about how impossibly useless March feels. Sort of like Mondays. Just wipe them off the calendar all together. Then here is where the dominos fell...

Domino 1: It reminded me of another annoying dry spell. The terribly boring time that starts just after college basketball and stretches until the NFL draft. There are no good sports for months. Unless you have a special year where the World Cup or Summer Olympics break up the monotony.

Domino 2: I guess I could get into baseball, but I don't have the patience to watch one game for seven hours. I have better things to do with my time. I have to go to work and shower and eat and look at Pinterest.

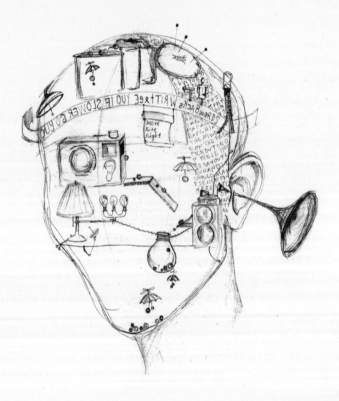

Domino 3: I'll just find out when the World Series is and tune in for that. This always works. I've done it for lots of other things. You ignore or avoid for months and then at the last minute throw your hat in the ring like you're some big fan whose been dying for a championship since you were three. I'm a sucker for a good showdown, but I don't like to wait out all the buildup beforehand. Just tell me when the total knockout is about to happen and I'll stand on the ropes. Yeah, that's what I'll do, I'll get the World Series schedule and rest up for that.

Domino 4: This is exactly what my life feels like. I woke up years after some terrible slumber and find myself in some sort of playoff series that I'm ill-equipped to participate in. Oh God, these people look familiar and even the field we're playing on. Everything smells and shakes in a way that feels appropriate and right, but it's all tainted with a foreign accent acquired from too much time away. Everyone knows the rules to the game. They all have the right equipment and have lingo and special hand signals to give each other shortcuts or warnings. They are organized and conditioned well. They remembered to stretch and tie their shoes and drink lots of water. And me? I feel like I went to bat with a bendy straw and I'm wearing a colander for a helmet.

And I know where first base is but for some awful reason I take off running to third base. And I know who my coach is, but I go pull a fan from the bleachers and ask him for advice instead. Somehow I missed all the buildup and prep work for this game. Like the most massively wrong turn I can think of. What's stranger is that almost everyone else out here doesn't seem to notice that I'm so lost. They just keep playing the game and overlook my often pathetic attempts. Is my name even on that roster or are they just letting me play to placate me? The way we let my four-year-old cousin "play" scrabble with us. "Yes, good job, Gzotr is absolutely a word and you get quadruple points! Now since you won the game you go outside and play."

Sometimes people tell me that "everyone does that" or "that's a totally human thing to think or say." And for a lot of cases I do believe this, but there are some things I think or do that I know are not "normal" and I wonder why people lie to me about this. Sometimes people really close to me won't lie to me and this feels so good. Someone else sees the shrapnel! I didn't imagine it! I'm not playing by myself! I get why I don't hear the weird truth a lot, people think they're being nicer by not naming it. But it is inside my head, it is in my fiber, a portion of me that I can't get rid of, can't heal, can't cut out. So to call it other names feels like lying to me. If I or they or we can rename the ugly part so easily, then what's to stop us from accidentally renaming the pretty part? What if we already have? What if I renamed someone accidentally?

Domino 5: I heard that God gives us a new name when we get to heaven. Holy shit! Why isn't this one of the first things they tell you in church? "God made heaven and earth, Jesus died on the cross, tithes go in the box, AND YOU GET A NEW NAME!" I like my physical name, "Tessie." I think it is befitting me and has a nice sound to it. But the shit on my soul. The names scrolled there, those ones go away and I get a new one. The one that God has known me by. The one He put on his roster. The name that if I heard it right now I would not recognize its sound or meaning. You wouldn't give a baby a wedding dress; God won't give me some gifts until I get up there. I'm too little to have some things on earth.

But I do "waiting" really poorly. I get caught up in the fact that I'm really behind and have a lot to learn. I wonder if it's all worth learning? I decide that it is not (without asking for a second opinion) and start crossing things off the proverbial list just to pare it down to a reasonable size. "Eat, shower, work, sleep, see people," that's what's left on the list. The longer I drink, the shorter the list gets and the harder it becomes to get to normal. The longer I am crazy the shorter the list gets. Some days all that is on there is "work and sleep" or sometimes just "sleep." Or sometimes it's "pretend to sleep so that you can pretend to wake up and then pretend to know what in the hell is going on." I want my new name.

The name I hate the most is "damaged." I am well aware that most of the names I have written in scar tissue on my soul are ones that I put there myself. The ones like "drunk," "addict," "selfish," "discontented." But the ones that got there without my knowledge or permission are the ones that really make earth feel like eternity. I don't like the fatherless feeling. I don't like the couple of names that I could have had in the future but now feel stolen because of my past. Or stolen because of the way my mind is wired. The wife and mother names. Those sweet names feel almost laughable. And to be quite honest, it doesn't help when someone says, "You might change your mind, you might get married yet. You might be a mother later in life!" Their hopeful optimism does little to quell the enormous loss of what it means to be a woman right now. The woman I am right now is often clueless and childish and so afraid. More names that I can't wait to have taken off. More names that Jesus promised He made room for and made payment for.

Domino 6: This church lady said that we are the "hope of glory." For the most part, I have no idea what she wanted this to mean when she said it with her lips. But when I said it with my lips I felt really haunted. I felt audacious and demanding

and arrogant and so desperate for it to be true. Am I really the
hope of Christ's glory? Would He put such stock in a fetid,
imploding mess like myself? Like if I had to choose a student
to go represent our class at the district meeting would I send
my A+ student who nearly does a curtsy when addressing
authority *or* I would send the jackass that I spend all class
period asking to "please behave like a normal human being"?
It seems so obvious, but if Christ calls me His hope of glory
then it really means He sent the barely human to reach and
love the other humans. Sometimes (actually a lot of times,
but "sometimes" seemed a lot softer) I really think Jesus came
up with the worst possible plan and instead of scrapping this
and starting over He just keeps trying to make it work. Like
at some point someone would say, "Hey Jesus, this idea sucks,
the humans are not understanding and they're making it
worse," but nobody told Him that He was out of his mind.
They just kept letting Him be God on the off chance that He
wasn't joking. That He was serious about using delinquents
to minister to other delinquents. That He really thinks it's a
good and decent thing to love people in the really shattered
condition they are. Poor Jesus. I bet He got picked on a lot
as a kid.

Winter

When most things die they look like they're dying. It is a gray mood and quiet and still. When leaves die, they get beautiful and colorful and they look like they're coming to life, but really they are dying. And for a couple of weeks we forget how hot we were in the summer and how terribly cold it gets during the winter. We forget because the leaves come to life and we remember how nice it feels to breathe cool air and wear sweatshirts and drink warm drinks with both hands around the mug. Things feel invigorated and the lively death of the world outside seems to be a rebirthing. Then without much warning at all, those beautiful leaves are all brown and crackle along the cement and the barren trees look a lot like skeletal fingers groping from the earth. The earth that both gave the leaves and now takes the leaves just because she tilts on her axis and on a whim the world is cold and shivers in response to her massive mood swing.

It's cold and windy and the sun goes to hide up in the galaxy much sooner than it used to. I feel tired long before bedtime and there is very little that motivates me to leave the sanctuary of the warm house. I let cabin fever settle in and linger like smoke. At first I can breathe under the smoke and occupy myself momentarily, but it builds quickly and in a few short weeks it is suffocating and I cannot remember what the thick August heat felt like.

In late November I am sitting on my couch and wishing some fairy would come in here with a cup of tea and some slippers. I am thinking about those leaves that just a couple of weeks ago were red and orange and yellow. Colors that were dramatic and loud and begged to be looked at. Now, they are all gone. They are all ugly and all over the place and I think winter looks more like the leftovers than it does the beautiful work of God. Everything feels scarce and holed up and people forget they need to leave the house. Winter feels like dying and it doesn't gradually settle in like the smoke of boredom or complacency, winter comes in short order. For as dormant and drowsy as I think it is, winter actually has a hurried agenda and comes with abruptness and stealth. Things have to die and winter comes to do this deed. If those leaves don't go away then they don't get to come back at all. If there was no death of them then they would simply go from buds to shriveled cocoons that never held the promise of color and life. The crumpled, wrinkled brown leaves would just cling lifelessly to the branches. Nothing new would grow there because the dead thing just takes up too much space.

I have dead things that cling to spaces meant for new things. There are parts of me that I know have died or are dying and I let the corpses pile up and stay in my soul because I hope against hope that they will resurrect and I'll sigh with relief that I didn't discard them too hastily. Things that on the surface look both good and bad. Like that red autumn leaf looks so gorgeous in mid-October that I would never consider it to be the same ugly, snarled one that I will find a few weeks later. When things are beautiful on the surface it is hard to imagine that dying is appropriate for them. When things are obviously ugly, it is a little easier to give them up to death. But even the ugly ones, when they are in your soul, feel terribly comfortable and that's when it becomes difficult to distinguish red leaves from brown leaves. That's when it feels traumatic to let things die and wither and blow away.

Red leaf: I want to fall in love. On the surface, this sounds fairly normal and sweet. What girl doesn't crave this? After all, didn't God create us to be in intimate relationships with each other? Wasn't I created to be yoked to and led by a righteous man? Wasn't I made to love sacrificially and selflessly? Wouldn't love cure my loneliness and longing to know my worth and dignity as a woman? Wouldn't marriage bring me to a clearer understanding of how Christ loves the church?

These are nice thoughts, and these are thoughts that I have really had. But what I also think about is that falling in love would silence the incessant whispering that says, "They are all the same, and he will hurt you." That loving a man will corner and cover the ghosts of men from my past. That a loving man will give me value. This pretty red leaf just turned into a big deception. Then on some days, like a winter day where dead things get blown away, I think more realistically.

Right now, today, my God-given truth is that my dignity has been restored and I may not understand this until I get to heaven. I may not understand and feel the evidence of that dignity until I see Jesus and He tells me He fixed that. But here, I might live with this blotted reality and I know and understand this is not marriage material. I may meet men who are righteous and loving, but today if I met him I would

not know how to look him in the eyes, never mind love him.
When I feel ashamed for even thinking about the fantasy of
falling in love, it then feels necessary that winter blow this
away. I'd rather just have this dying thing be pulled off the
limb and taken away instead of it flapping around awkwardly.

Brown leaf: I wish my solution were as easy as drinking.
Oh God, take this one. This painfully obvious dead thing. Take
this relentless notion, this hideous insanity. This thing that sits
in the room with me and in a dry, liquor-less home makes me
believe that drinking is a plausible and rational idea. A right
and wise idea. This thing that lays in bed with me, cozy under
the covers, and reenacts the nightmares of yesterday. The
thing that makes me anxious about driving, about grocery
shopping, about being alone, about being in a group, about
being in my skin. The thing that makes me cower behind fear
and then erupt in irrational anger. This leaf has got to go,
but it feels like such a part of my fiber that it feels insincere
to exist without it. This brown leaf flits around and mocks
me and avoids the death of winter. Without a winter that I
participate in, this leaf may endure for a long time.

THE COLDEST WINTER I'VE BEEN in was in Boone, North
Carolina. I was doing my undergraduate studies; or rather I
was attending class semi-conscious and hung-over for about
two years. Those winters make people reconsider the well-
loved notion that hell is hot because it may in fact be an icy
abyss. I remember walking to class in two feet of snow and
the wind chill pushed the temperature to 30 below 0. This
is the type of cold that freezes the blood in your fingers and
toes and coldness really acts as an anesthesia. You just keep
walking along like this is perfectly normal, like most days are

spent regaining feeling in your lower extremities. The cold nights keep you indoors and in hot showers and sitting on top of dryers. Drinking heavily felt justified, lest my blood stop flowing and I freeze to death. This is the type of winter that magnifies the really simple things and everything else is willingly cast aside: not even counted as lost luxuries, but simply unnecessary and undeserving of my effort or attention.

When I was the most cold and most trapped by winter I felt most satisfied by a warm blanket, a warm meal and a warm room. All the extras and addendums that come with warmer months seemed silly and rather pointless. Just give me that warm blanket, close the door, and let the winter blow the rest to little pieces. When I was the most desperate in my life, the most caught up in the winter of my soul, I still wanted the same precious things that I wanted in the physical winters of Boone. I want a blanket, a meal, and a place to go to sleep safely. I wanted the warmth and comfort of knowing there was a refining and simplifying going on and I just had to wait out the storm. Prayer becomes sacred in these types of winters. In desperation, prayer seems to be the last remaining thing I am capable of. Even when I am convinced the winter was ordained and planned and this makes me angry and bitter at the god who orchestrated it, I still cry out to Him as I curse Him. These winters feel painful and cruel, but when it's really still and quiet they almost feel necessary. The way fire refines metal, the coldness clears out the dead things and makes way for what should really be there.

Blindside

From my blindside,
You got me.
Total knockout from the ring.
And I can bob and weave all night, and still bruise.
Because you still lose,
You can still lose.
From the backdoor,
You snuck in.
Quiet darkness from the locked room.
And I can duck and hide all night, and still cry.
Because you still die,
You can still die,
From the inside.
You slept there.
Just a mirror and a lie of the same thing.
And I can pretend and run all night, and still know,
Because you still win.
Sinful man, you still win.

I Threw Jesus under the Bus

I teach a bunch of teenagers and on any given day someone gets in trouble for a really stupid thing and then blatantly and ruthlessly shoves the blame onto whoever they are sitting beside. Passing a dirty note, throwing things, slamming the door, and on and on. I will ask the perpetrator why they did whatever the infraction happens to be and every single time it is the same answer, "It wasn't me!" And because I sometimes turn into a psycho tyrant in my classroom, I *need* to know who did it. I need someone to punish. So sometimes I get the right kid and sometimes I punish the wrong kid all because his idiot friend blamed Him for it.

When I believe my students are the spawn of Satan, it is really painful and hard to see that I'm just like them. Oh, what a crushing blow to be a grown woman and know that I'm no better off than a 15-year-old jerk. As an "adult" I continuously look for people or things or secret places to shift blame away from me so that I can pretend to be less screwy than I really am. The stupid thing is that I do this for really trivial, insignificant things. The big shit is hard to cover up, so I claim that real quick. But the little stuff, the incessant, daily sins that could easily be overlooked in light of the massive ones. The little ones that seep into crevices and lay dormant for years. The little ones that nobody else senses or sees or experiences. The little ones that merit little attention simply because they are inconspicuous. The little ones that collect and gain momentum until they are suddenly large and I'm shocked and say, "Where the hell did this come from?"

As a Christian, I'm supposed to believe that Jesus came to get people who needed getting. People who couldn't fix themselves and who wouldn't fare very well in front of a judging god. I'm supposed to believe that Jesus' inherent goodness takes the place of my inherent humanness. There has to be judgment, there has to be a price paid. Someone will shoulder the blame and if it's not me individually accounting for my life, then I'm supposed to throw Jesus under the bus and let Him take the heat.

I really hope, for all parties involved, that God doesn't turn out to be the psycho that I sometimes am in my classroom. That would be a supreme bummer. But, as strange as this sounds, I do think there is some similarity in the *need* for payment. No one gets to be human and live in a broken world and then claim Christ and then gets off scot-free. I wish that were the case, but there has to be a payment. Either from my end or from Jesus'. To God, psycho or not, the payment will be collected. The idea of using Christ as a buffer seems so stupid that I am actually sitting here laughing (silently) to myself. This is what I'm picturing… God sitting on His cloud at the border crossing into heaven. I picture Him sort of sitting like those Buddha statues, He's not Buddha, He just happens to be sitting like him. And He is saying "covered" or "not covered" to each person at the border. They are either covered by the insurance and scheme of Christ, or they are not. Then I picture Jesus literally standing in my place and God says, "covered," while I'm hiding in the bushes whispering, "Yessss! Fooled the old man again!" And He must not have very good eyesight or He must not care, but either way He doesn't seem to notice that He's accepted Jesus into heaven billions of times.

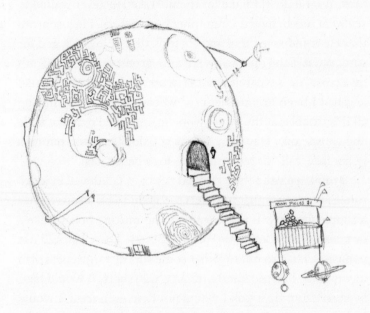

I am a terrible Christian on many, many fronts. However, I am really good at two things: I understand the idea of "payment" really well and I understand the need to be saved.

Item #1: I totally grasp that my behavior and decisions will have repercussions for a long, long time. The horror of some things will echo around my head for my entire life; that is the cost I pay. This is a heavy, burdensome payment to make so I can't imagine what it would be after I die. How much worse would an eternal debt be? I can't calculate that. But apparently, this is the debt that I'm excused from because of Jesus. No wonder people think Jesus is stupid...what an unfair deal. Sometimes I think Jesus jumped at the offer to save humanity a little too fast. Who knows, maybe God was going to give a few options and He could have picked the best one, but since Jesus was so in love He just freaked out and said, "Yes! Yes, I'll do it! I'll die for them!" Like He never waited to see what was behind door number two or three, He just heard that He could save them and He took that. A lovesick god for sure. What if the options were "die a gruesome, public death on a cross" or "go barefoot for 80 years"? I'm a betting woman and had I been in Jerusalem (or wherever Jesus was making all this trouble) at the time I would have leaned over the table and whispered, "Hey man, I think you double down, put on a poker face, call His bluff and wait for a better deal."

I think it's safe to say I would not have fared well in Jesus' time. The truth is that my sin is too great to be forgiven with a simple apology. It is too grave to be making bets or dares or guesses. Jesus knew this, *knows* this. He knew I would not make it if I had to put together some sort of forgiveness plan of my own. I would fall short. Way, way short. It would have been so daunting a task I would not have even tried, I would have just resigned to hell years before it was time. I gamble, even when I'm losing and then at the last crucial second I throw Jesus under the bus and it is suddenly redeemed.

Item #2: Desperate people travel lightly. The need to be saved is so massive that there is no strength to carry other needs or desires or wishes. And you look crazy, really bona fide insane, because you are desperate for something that you can't see and even if you get it, no one saw it delivered. I have spent many years defending myself against myself. A clever, sad, and slow suicide. Desperate to be freed from this mind, from this literal body that craves ruin. So, when I needed saving all I did was call out to Jesus. I didn't have things to gather, books to refer to, calls to make, errands to run. I was lying on a floor and begged. I had nothing, not by choice or virtue, but by circumstance.

But the scarcity and depravity of these circumstances are just perfect for saving. Jesus was sent to get people like this. In church they read the story of a crippled man and on a Sunday Jesus told him to pick up his bed and walk. And the man did; he stood up, picked up his bed and walked. This man was desperate and traveling lightly for sure. My guess is that it hadn't always been this way. Probably years and years before this, this man was laid up in some fancy hospital or some special church pew. He might have had sages and soothsayers and remedies and concoctions. He probably spent all his money trying to fix this or trying to ignore this. Then after years of this fruitless effort he is left with a filthy bed and he is still unable to walk.

For me, it's not the distraction of tangible things that get in the way of my desperation. It's me thinking I am strong enough, smart enough, capable of changing things. Thinking I can forget or erase or ignore. Thinking it will be different this time. It is arrogance and judgment. These are the things I hold before my willingness to beg for help. I live in this cycle and when the cycle is at the "empty" part then I'm traveling lightly and laid out, crippled, and broke. He'll tell me to get up, pick up my bed and walk. Walking is miraculous to a cripple, the same way that waking up is miraculous to a sinner.

Jesus is Annoying

I feel close to God under a few specific conditions. One, when I'm drunk. My guard is down and my ability to reason and logically catalog God is really interrupted. I feel bodily drunk but lucid in my spirit. I may die sober, but on my deathbed I will not be convinced that this is not the case. Condition two, when I listen to gospel music. Condition three, when I feel alone. Not alone like I haven't seen or talked to anyone for a few days or weeks (I do this all the time). I mean "alone" like I have exhausted all available resources here and this is as good as it gets and this reality is too hard. I feel close to God in this void because I again turn to Him as a last resort.

I am a piss poor follower. I would do really poorly in a cult. I'll be laying very still and staring into a dark room at some ungodly hour and wondering why this is the world God made. Wondering why Jesus would want to save something like this. Asking questions that sound a lot like profanity and distrust. Questions that teeter on blaming God and smacking His face because He can't possibly have intended for me to be this way. Right there, in that moment of disgust and hatred I remember that Jesus is a sad god. His heart hurts and the reflection of His sacrifice only trickles in slowly. I only know a few people that Jesus would be super excited about as they are now. As for the rest of us? Well, that's what makes Jesus annoying. I know with great certainty that I deserve punishment and blame, but I won't receive it. Then I have the audacity to wallow. I have been given a light at the end of the tunnel and as I trudge toward it I cry instead of rejoice. If Jesus wasn't righteous then I wouldn't feel so guilty. In a good solid week I think about Jesus in a right way about two times. The other times I think about Him I am angry and confused and hurt. I don't know what to pray or how to pray. I can't read the bible without frustration. I can't sit still long enough to do it anyway. I am not pious or devoted or confident in my belief. I am waiflike and shaky and afraid of commitment. This is a frail relationship I have with Christ. He seems pursuant and bold; I seem uninterested and rude. Is this really the greatest story ever told? Is this really the way mankind will be rescued? Is this really the example the world will follow? It is a strange world that my salvation hinges on a god that refuses to give up on a forgettable, lonely, scared little girl.

Mark 7 (or close to it)

The laws that I've made are so old and so routine that I wasn't even aware I'd made them in place of God's will. I was so accustomed to doing my righteous bill of rights that even when something more sacred came along, I was unable to recognize it because my way was so familiar. If tomorrow they made a law that red lights meant "go" I guarantee that I would stop at every single red light and plow through the green ones simply because that was what I was used to. From black to white. I think that is what the Pharisees must have felt when Jesus came to town. Rules and laws and stipulations and caveats and loopholes and all of it made complete sense until Jesus shook the shit to pieces. Like trying to explain the intersection of Queens and Queens to someone who isn't from Charlotte. Or why we call downtown "uptown."

I just learned that there are about five million versions of the bible, but in the version I read it said that the old souls of Jerusalem "clung to" their traditions. I get this. I understand this. I was raised to cling to and sew my fabric to traditions regardless of their validity. Exhibit A: Every Christmas Eve we go to a Catholic mass at 11pm so that when the service is done it is very technically Christmas. We don't go to church any other day of the year, but this tradition is as sacred as turkey on Thanksgiving. Exhibit B: Keep a secret. I taught myself the delicate practice of keeping a secret. To stuff the carpet with secrets and unsavory things that just shouldn't hit the public domain...even though all parties involved knew that all other parties involved already knew the details. The big idea was not to give voice to it. I imagine the Pharisees would have welcomed me with open arms upon hearing my valiant efforts to keep the status quo. People who don't break code, who don't override tradition, who don't supersede rank or age or myth.

Then right when all seems to be going as planned... Jesus busts the shit up. Comes up in the place with his idiot "disciples" who don't have the sense to wash their hands and who go around acting like total barbarians. I would have been pissed! I would have been like, "Man! I kept all these secrets! I kept all these lies in balance; I did all this bullshit and for what? For you and your moron gang to come over here and mess it all up?" Because the truth is that it takes skill and talent and effort to sidestep the will of God and before Jesus I was successful at doing so. All my diligence paid off up until the point that God was man. Because He shows up and my sobriety, my purity, my silence, my blind eye are all to shit. They mean nothing if they are consumed, digested, and discarded like food. They are the foolish laws of self-righteous Pharisees. Those things that looked so shiny and so new to my eyes become dulled and lack-luster when Jesus asks me if they are from my heart.

I remember lying on the floor of a jail cell and realizing that Jesus was who He said He was. Up until this moment, Jesus was a stupid historical figure who somehow still lingered in the dreams of adult children. But at the moment that I calmly and semi-consciously realized Jesus was God, then everything became so obvious and so ugly. So obvious: why I sucked at life alone, why I couldn't stay sober, why I was broken and damaged and dying, why I was so tired, why I was suicidal and guilty. So ugly: why I was not enough, why I could not fix this alone, why even doing a good thing was not "my" good thing, why healing was in vain if it was my effort. Bittersweet would be the understatement of the year. The Pharisees, in the belly of their souls, had to know how bittersweet it was to see Jesus screwing up their laws. Their lips said pretty things while their hearts fouled it up. The aftertaste of their hearts ruined the sweetness of their words. I can relate to this. Sometimes I regret having to forget the immediate knowledge of that jail cell. How easy it was to know Jesus as God. How easy it was to be vulnerable and be judged by my actions and not my words. How simple it was to lie on a floor and beg to Christ for salvation not for eternity, but for the salvation of one single day. How petty and silly the laws of the jail seemed in light of what Jesus could say inside a single cell. Because I can promise you it wasn't the eloquence of my prayer that got Jesus to weep, but rather the hopelessness of my heart.

The Jumping Off Place

He cannot picture life without alcohol. Some day he will
be unable to imagine life either with alcohol or without
it. Then he will know loneliness such as few do. He will
be at the jumping-off place. He will wish for the end.

Alcoholics Anonymous, p. 152

Here is the jumping off place. The place where inching into
the grave is comfortable, inevitable and charming. The place
where backing away slowly from the belly of a beast is at best
a snowball's chance in hell. The line between the two begins
to blur and becomes indiscriminate. Choices and decisions
seem to make themselves because of one choice you made
17 years prior. Teetering between an easy out and what other
humans seem to tackle with impunity. You come to terms
with the fact that you were born this way and, fate being
unchanging, must die this way. The blows are easier to take if
you come to grips with the reality of it. You pride yourself for
being aware and accepting of your lot. You hunker down in a

cradle of shit and pray to a god you know must be laughing. At that jumping off place you lay down and wait *or you move.*

From where I sit now, it appears I moved off and down from the edge. It likely appears factual and assured from others' perspectives that yes, indeed, I have ventured far from the jumping off place because the obvious monster has been removed. From inside my head the jumping off place lingers just over my shoulder as though in six months of traveling I've only moved two feet. The monster hovers and groans painfully from behind me. Begging for attention, promising relief, reminding me of the easy out that would come swiftly and quietly. I move forward, ever slowly, from the tipping point, all the while grieving the loss of the monster. Statistically, of the 20 women I lived with for five months, 18 of them will go back to the wasteland. That same god I found in my defilement now ceases to laugh and simply weeps for the utter loss of lovely things.

I GET AHEAD OF MYSELF. Most stories start at the beginning. The end of this story is so lucid and unbound that it sat heavy and untimely at the beginning of the tale. Seventeen years ago I took a Coors Light up to the attic of my mother's house. The attic was cooler and darker and I could be alone. Looking back, the attic mimicked the bars I would frequent many years later. I drank that single beer and as its magic radiated from my throat to sternum and down to my fingertips, I said *out loud* to the can, "You are my new best friend." This my friends is what observant humans call a "red flag." It's too bad that flag got swallowed up; otherwise I could have saved myself a lifetime of annihilation.

But as a 13-year-old kid I wasn't on the lookout for any more obstacles or warnings, I was looking for relief and that can of rank-tasting beer provided and paved the way. And I knew that something this potent needed to be kept secret. A nuclear warhead stashed away in the mothballs of the attic. The secret kept quiet wasn't that I was eight years shy of the legal drinking age and it wasn't that I stole the beer. The secret was that if more people in my immediate vicinity knew what I'd stumbled across then they too would use up the secret and there would be less for me. This single moment in my life would be the pinnacle one that I tried in vain to replicate for 17 years.

Every alcoholic sip I took after the attic was in an attempt to recapture the complete relief and joy that surfaced when I was 13. Nearly every sip would be done in cold, dark, lonely places. In secret. In anticipation and anxious waiting. In places and times that drinking was the least appropriate thing. And although I believed it was aiding me for years and years, that aluminum can would never reciprocate the sold-out devotion I heaped upon it. That "best friend" in the attic met me and then turned on a heel and began a 17-year suicide. Before you go thinking, how was a kid supposed to know it unleashed a man-eating beast in the attic, isn't it sad and epic? ...let me tell you that pity has saved exactly zero alcoholics. I do believe there is a great and ugly misunderstanding about the alcohol problem, but to be clear, I am not recounting mine to secure charity and pity. My addiction may very well be genetic in part, but it is one of the very few diseases that is activated and put into remission by *conscious choices*. In the throes of addiction, it is true that choice is lost, but there will come a jumping off place that is offered multiple times to every single addict. Lie down and wait or move. I laid down for so long.

The Comfort of Darkness

I'm 30 years old now and still waiting for myself to muster the resolve to confidently walk away from my addiction. Some nights I am convinced that there is hope and all will improve with slow and deliberate paces forward. That good things will fall into place if I simply do what is decent and right, right now. Other nights, I stomach the undeniable truth that I will be a miserable dry drunk for the rest of my life. The wealth of contentment just out of reach for a lifetime. That this really is the best it will be, so get used to it.

Then like a bubble surfacing from an oily mixture, the thought occurs to me that there is a third option. An option not like the water of sobriety and not like the oil of desperation, but in and of itself a rude and sudden burp of air emerging between the two that says I could drink and die and all of this would be done. It begs to be considered among the choices. It is the loudest option, literally calling out to me. It registers on all levels and speaks a language that I often only hear and understand when I'm consumed in the comfort of darkness. When I am well and moving in any right direction, the third option is audible, but it sounds like a muffled idiot crying out in tongues I don't quite comprehend. But when I am crawling around low in my head and my chest feels concave with depression, that same babbling idiot speaks clearly and dare I say wisely.

And here is the part that feels so absurdly stupid to me. There is one section of the blob of gray matter in my brain that computes logical things and it will always say, "Drinking is a conscious choice." Then there is another blob that refutes the factual and lives completely off of irrational emotion and he says, "When I am so fractured and unwilling to live, there are no choices." How can one brain say these two things?

Which is true and which is a finely dressed lie masquerading as valid advice? I bounce between the two, dizzy with contempt and anger.

I would feel afraid to know that someone close to me thinks in this black and white, binary manner. But with myself, I feel grateful for days that seem to work well while simultaneously remembering that one fine day I may very well drink myself into oblivion. Sad? No, not sad. More like longing. There are crooked, broken things in me that no drink, no drug, no earthly thing will stitch up. I long to be let go by my mind. I can imagine with stark clarity what dying would mean. The odd combination of things that I have been given, that you have been given, that all of us have been given will finally add up to something meaningful. And not just sporadically useful and purposeful, but perfect and synchronized as they never could be alive.

Dying is so ugly on the earth side. But how elegant and captivating on the north side of things. I imagine with clear eyes that I and we will not have a definition for what we once referenced as "alcoholism." That the oddities of my mind will settle. And most of all I see us groping to understand what we called "depression." We will not know these things. What a divinely beautiful thing. I think maybe we endure a little longer with such bright prospects.

One Thing Goes

I wait for one thing to change. One thing that will set a domino effect into motion. One small, subtle thing. One thing that is truth because I didn't orchestrate it. I didn't manipulate and bargain for it. I didn't grovel at the foot of some idol. I simply waited, for 30 years. And the waiting was graceless and full of shame and ugly decisions. It was crooked and aimless for the most part. It was without reward or favor and without surety or promise. It had peaks of joy and laud, but the downward slope that followed quickly overcame the peaks. The one thing was so less profound than I thought it would be, than I hoped for. It was so much less miraculous and momentous than I fantasized about. It was so damn subtle that I would certainly have missed it had I not been sitting still in the company of someone who cried with me. With someone who did not condescend me by asking me why I was crying. She either already knew or she didn't need to know. I was sitting and crying silently. I'm not even sure I knew what I was crying over, but it mattered none. Three decades rushed the room and begged for forgiveness. And then, then the one thing changed. The thing = my perspective. I realized for the first time in my life, that at that moment, it was over. It was all over and done with. I had survived and I had beat the very poor odds. It was over. I said it out loud. She said it back to me as though it were her revolution too.

"It's all over, it's done."

"It's done."

"I'm still alive and it's over."

"You are alive, I can't believe it."

"I cannot believe it's over."

"It's over."

I believed that the very bad, long storm was over and that none of its episodes needed to be repeated or played out again. All my life I witnessed the same horrific and labor-intensive scenes replay and replay ad nauseam. It was with my permission and effort and it was sometimes simply the momentum of the downward slope that steamrolled me. It was impossible to stop and impossible to reroute. But then I believed it was all one very large chunk of time that I had lived through and was now done with. The credits rolled up on this one and the last 30 years were done.

As I sat there crying I couldn't figure out why I wasn't jumping for joy, why my face was not obviously showing signs of relief. Why didn't these tears feel like tears of joy? Why didn't I feel less heavy? I did feel immensely relieved and unburdened, but my face looked like a funeral. This is what tragic relief looks like I suppose. Like going into surgery without enough anesthesia. They gave you enough to make you look like you're asleep, but not enough to curb physical feeling. Gritting your teeth for a few hours just begging and screaming for them to stop, but no one can hear you because you're not actually making any noise. And then it does stop, when the surgery is over, you are elated because you survived, but the price of survival is a steep one that haunts. This is how I felt, I think. It felt like the 30 years were being neatly packed away and out of arm's reach. Like I was given a sworn affidavit that it would not be duplicated. Like sweet, miraculous relief, but the shock of it washes up on you and you celebrate birth while you mourn a million tiny deaths. Oh, the dead things that one by one were being packed away. The cost of them incalculable, but dead as bones rattling underground as though they never lived at all. The sedation of just keeping your head above water wears off and you look around and survey the damage and marvel that anything breathes at all.

As I sat there crying, I thought of Jesus and He nodded in response and agreement when I said out loud that it was all over. He knew it too, and I realized He'd been waiting for this marker in time too. He'd been gritting His teeth too and wailing when time seemed to crawl, when it looked hopelessly worthless. And I think He cried too. The best therapy I've ever had was when someone cried with me. That is an acknowledgment far deeper than any intimacy I've ever experienced. Jesus has a lot to cry about, but even though our faces looked like funerals that day, we both knew we were crying for the great relief I'd been promised.

To my surprise this shift in perspective didn't involve any form of retaliation or revenge, which is what I had long hoped my redemption would include. It didn't have any taint of vigilante or merciless justice. It was free of the things that I had dreamed up and it was full of things that a good god puts in the place of my fantastic, fatalistic ideas.

Collect from County

Recently a friend asked me how I knew I was an alcoholic. I knew immediately the real purpose of the question. It wasn't an exercise it getting to know each other. It wasn't curiosity or concern. It was because the person suspected the ugly truth about themselves was that they too had a drinking problem and needed a baseline test to conduct on themselves. To prove once and for all that they were or were not a lush. Like testing the waters on a phantom guinea pig. You know the way, "A friend of mine might have problem XYZ, what do you think?" We go around our elbows to get to our asses. But this is the nature of struggling. The nature of denial and self-reliance.

So when this friend asks me, it's painfully obvious to me that they are essentially asking me to compare my drinking career to their own. I weigh my options carefully. I immediately think of a couple anecdotes that demonstrate my propensity for drunkenness very well. I briefly tell her about when I got arrested and I called my job collect because it was the only landline number that I knew, because this information is mostly funny to non-alcoholics but to alcoholics it is funny and typical. I tell her about a friend of mine (this story really is about a friend of mine, I'm not doing the old switch-a-roo I just complained about) who during her addiction used to soak cigarettes in vodka then let them dry out. She'd then smoke the vodka cigarettes during work breaks for a quick head rush. Upon hearing this story, most humans do not know how to respond to the utter psycho-ness of her efforts. When I heard this story I thought she was clever and innovative beyond even what Bill Gates had orchestrated. I thought how genius she was and what a shame I'd never thought of it. I thought she was a prodigy of some sort that would likely take over the world by the end of the week. If you think the vodka cigarette is a viable and new niche market, then you are probably alcoholic. And I get it. No one wants this label.

Oh for the love of God, diagnose me with a debilitating mental illness before you condemn me to a life of sobriety. "Alcoholic" pulls up a strong mental picture for most folks as it does for me, and to this day, I still hold stereotypes about alcoholics and they never look like me. I ask my friend the standard questions that four million therapists and program gurus have asked me. Questions that I think are unfair and not thoroughly researched because if you are only having two drinks at a sitting then you are probably pregnant or something. What is "normal" and "not normal" are laughably different in my world. I tell my friend about how going to Panera Bread is hard because the yeast smells just like beer to me. How being too happy or too sad or too stressed or too relaxed are all triggers for drinking. How driving seems so irritating now that I don't have a beer in the cup holder. How the smell of a lime makes my mouth water and my stomach ache because all I can think about is tequila. My friend looks at me with a face that is both horrified and amused. Horrified maybe because she relates to this sickness of mind and it feels like a death sentence because there is no escaping it. Amused maybe because I sound like an idiot and from the outside I probably have looked like an idiot for much of my life, but without laughing at some of it I would succumb to tears. A lot was lost in my addiction. A lot will never be recovered or repaired. But I made it out with my sense of humor intact and that has helped to stomach the blows of loss.

My friend eases a little bit and I think it's because she feels like I'm her "porch." A quiet spot, 72 degrees and sunny. A nice cool breeze, nothing to do but sit in a rocking chair, sip coffee, and talk to someone who perhaps lives in this very comfortable and familiar home. I have a lot of porch people in my life. I decide to tell her the full story about getting arrested just to cement the porch feeling. She'll know for sure that she isn't alone after hearing this.

One fine spring evening I decided to go to one of my two favorite bars. This one happened to be on the other side of town from my apartment, which was fine by me because I lived in a notorious crack neighborhood and I used bar drinking as a valid excuse to avoid my home. I also used weather and time and conspiracy theories as reasons for drinking. But that's beside the point. So there I was remaining safe by going to the bar outside the ghetto. I was drinking tequila and chasing with light beer. I stopped counting shots after 11 because the math was too hard. Algebra is so tedious when you are drunk.

At some point I decided I needed to go home because I had to go to work the next day. I was working two jobs at this point and my day job was a regular people schedule of 9 to 5. People didn't show up drunk or hung-over and they were freshly showered and perky. I needed to get home to sober up before sunrise. As I turned out of the parking lot I managed to take a direct hit on the curb that may or may not have been put there during the time I was in the bar. At any rate, when you hit a curb at 30 mph it tends to shred your tires off and crumple your rims like they were made of tin foil. But I kept driving because I only had 20 miles or so to go. There were large waves of sparks spewing like the Fourth of July from my car where the tinfoil rims were grinding on the road. I turned on my hazard lights to warn other drivers that there was something amiss with my car and they shouldn't get too close.

After about a mile or so I saw the blue lights in my rearview mirror and my very first thought was, "Oh thank God, these officers can help me get home." I had no idea I was in trouble. I knew I was drunk driving. I knew I should not be driving. I knew I was an alcoholic, but none of this mattered. When the cop came to my window he asked if I'd been drinking and since alcohol has always been a sort of truth serum to me, I blurted out with a little giggle that yes, I had been drinking a lot. He asked how much and I said I had no idea. He took me out of the car, handcuffed me and sat me in the grass to wait. I still had no idea that things were not going well, so I took it upon myself to ask the police officer for a cigarette while I waited in the grass. He obliged and lit me a cigarette that I smoked with sheer delight. I did some field sobriety tests for him and to his surprise, I was able to complete them. He gave me three Breathalyzer tests because it did not seem possible that my blood alcohol content should be so high and I still be conscious. On my drive over to county jail the officer (whose name was pronounced "beer" but spelled with some German flair) asked if I thought I had a drinking problem. I told him that I did have one and I distinctly remember thinking it was a stupid question but how freaking awesome that his name was "beer."

I do not remember much of the next 48 hours. Two days completely wiped out by drunken stupor and withdrawal. I do remember waking up on the floor of a cell and I was wearing a green, Velcro dress that was made for people of normal sizes...not for six-feet-tall girls. I felt naked and cold and impossibly confused. It was all cement. The walls, the floor, the ceiling, the bench that was to serve as my bed. The only soft things were the Velcro dress and the toilet water. It was a suicide cell and the lights were kept on 24 hours a day. It was cold and it was so, so lonely. I remember standing up and vomiting. I remember looking out the little window in the door and realizing that all the girls in this unit were pregnant and then I stared in disgust at my own body believing the warden knew something I did not. I would later find out that this was a "special population" unit, aka all the inmates were pregnant weekenders, and the suicide cell was housed here because it was the calmest unit.

What I said or did to land in that cell I still have no idea. I believe I wound up there because my blood alcohol content was so high that they must have known I was an alcoholic and losing it. And I did lose it. I laid on the floor and felt a soft, soft rain falling on my face. It was raining inside the cell and it was amazing. It felt clean and healthy and right. I remember praying to Jesus that He would burn down the county jail. I literally told Him that I didn't care if we all burned up in the fire, but that we could not be in here anymore. God does not like homicidal prayers, so instead of a great fire, He fooled my mind into believing there was a great rainstorm inside the cell.

I could *hear* the rain, feel it on my skin, smell its dewiness. It wasn't the pitter-patter like on a roof, but the soft sound of sheets blowing. It got louder each time I closed my eyes, so I kept my eyes shut for the first time in two days. I laid on the cement bench quietly and completely still, imagining that I was lying outside in the soaking rain.

When my mind came back to me a few days later I realized that it wasn't actually raining that night. I'm not sure what the sound was, but it was raining in my head. I remember feeling sure that the fact that I was in jail was deserved and just, but I really had no idea why I was in the suicide cell. I wasn't suicidal, but desperation looks a lot like dying when it's all consuming. To other people, active addiction almost always looks like suicide.

It occurred to me that "normal" people don't wake up in jail cells hallucinating. In fact most people, I imagine, hallucinate *with* substances, but my body hallucinates when there is an absence of them. I began to hope that this was a bottom. I had long heard that addicts do not recover until they reach their bottom. I had experienced so many nights that I was sure were my bottom and that a new life would begin the next day. But inevitably there was always a loose floorboard waiting to collapse to let me fall to my next bottom. Like a skyscraper with 50 floors and each floor breaks through like a cartoon and I continue to smack to the next lower level making a spread eagle cut-out on each floor and ceiling that I plow through.

This bottom was different. It had to be. Not because it was the worst consequence, or the most shameful, or the most hellish. But because this bottom had no escape. What I remember most vividly is being very cold and very tired and very hungry. The guards outside my tiny window regarded me as every other worthless drug addict they had ever come across, and their scorn was almost audible. They had blankets in their supply closet, but would not give me one. They had the ability to turn off the lights, but they left them on 24 hours a day. They had food, but my body revolted and I could not keep anything down. This was the most tangible demonstration of what my addiction looked like. How it had manifested so thoroughly in my life. I had no control in this cell. And I had no control on my own outside the cell. I had lost everything, including my mind. The guards, though just doing their jobs, represented a very clear picture of addiction. They withheld everything simple, basic, and good because I was deemed too sick or dangerous or mental to have those things. My addiction swallowed all things good and simple in my life because addiction has no reverence for worth.

It is a humbling thing to know that all you want in the whole world is a blanket and the lights turned off. I pounded the window with my fist, then arm, then shoulder until I was sore and bruised down the whole side. They would glance at me occasionally, but there was no movement toward the door. I resigned myself to the cement bench and trembled like a basket of clothes on top of a dryer. Then the sobbing. The wailing. The snapshots of all my consequences blurred before me. I was sobering up and had no choice but to look at these things. This is about the time, day two, that the "rain" started to fall outside. I decided it was time to pray. Or rather, it was time to pick up that last resort that I so stoically avoided for years.

ADDICTS WILL TELL YOU THAT a moment of clarity changes things. I believe I had several hundred moments of clarity in the past ten years, so I can't explain why this one meant something different. I've prayed before. I've cried before. I have said a thousand times that I would quit drinking and using drugs. It makes very little sense to me that being in jail would have had any persuasion. I also believe that I had to go there, that my God allowed that to happen, like so many other things that I have harbored anger over. But when I left jail I was not angry at God, I was not determined to drink the memory to oblivion. I didn't have a foolproof plan for recovery. I didn't know how I was going to keep myself from doing things that would land me right back in jail. I didn't even trust myself not to drink the moment I got home. But I did believe, sincerely believe, that I would not be able to do this alone. I prayed to a god to heal me and restore me and that presence was as sure as the cement bench. It felt completely ridiculous and absurd to believe in a god, but at the same time I had no reservations about it. I did not care if I looked idiotic for believing in God. At the very least I would be alive looking silly rather than dead with nothing of substance to leave.

It would be so satisfying to say that I left that cell and marched on to a sober life with ease and grace. But this is not reality. I did not expect God to take it all away like it had never been there in the first place. I expected very little from God because this was all that my little faith could sustain. I am not sober-go-lucky, but I am fortunate. I am alive, despite my best efforts to do otherwise. Some days I start over ten times before I catch my footing. Some nights I drive circles around this city for hours until I am calm. There is more to me than my mistakes. There is more to me than the nightmares I have seen and have created. There is infinitely more to me because God is infinitely more than me.

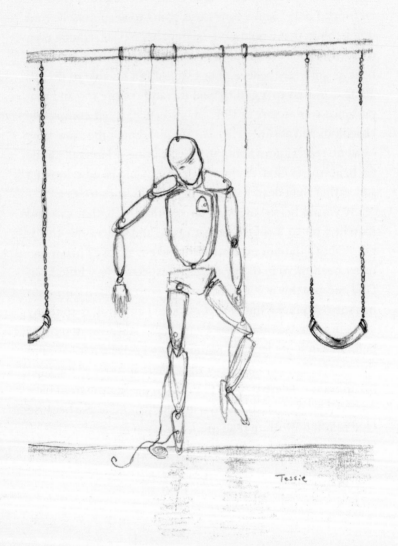

Tessie

Gone

I am the back street.
Across the tracks.
Wrong side.
Bad company.
Dark alley.
Smokey rooms.
I am the side street,
The well-armed and unaware,
Poorly lit and off the grid.
Blind eye turned,
Let it run its course.
Lost cause off the list.
I am the ugly part,
That's never cast, never shown.
The un-glorious
Un-victorious
Un-dead side of death.
I am the lovely thing eater

The life womb shaker
The good job snatcher
The pretty face scratcher.
A sweet song to silence.
A long laugh to jokes over.
Oh your young heart,
Hung by its old mind.
Stalemate. Round one.
No back tracking on a one-way,
No mercy in this stay.
No chance.
Last choice.
Tight rope.
End line.
Strung out.
Beat back.
Blind man.
Stone deaf.
Glory gone.
Time up.
Gone girl.
Gone.

Shame

Suddenly born and raised overnight,
I need no time to get this right.
I am so much your face and soul,
That the mirror will not notice my toll.
You'll wonder when I came.
When I overtook.
When I rearranged.
How I meddle so thoroughly.
Ruin so completely.
You will beg to rip me from your fiber,
But fail to find a loosened thread.
You will blame this on your genes.
On your sadness, on your age.
Condemn your inabilities.
Confess your sins.
You will call it sickness.
You will call me the product,
Of a broken, busted world.

You will give up.
Give up.
Resign.
Quit entirely.
They will find you withered and wonder,
Is this suicide or murder?
They will not blame me,
They will not chain me,
They will not condemn me.
They will not hunt me down like I did you.
They will let me go free,
To wander around unnamed.
Because they'll miss it just as you did.
That I'm so blatantly there,
So clearly, squarely in the forefront.
But you cannot see it.
Not then, not now.
You cannot see it.
Even in the unraveling,
You held up your chin.
Pretended like a child.
Afraid of the dark.
Cried out like a madman.
Clawed at the heavens.
But I am obese in my settling.
And lazy in leaving.
I am bigger and wider.
I am sadder.
I am more patient.
More creative in my injury.
I am more than you can overcome.
So you will give in.

And I will win again.
I will be let loose.
You will be hung.
You will cry out.
I will keep quiet.
You'll take me up like a cross to bear.
Yoke me to your soul to share,
Thinking this communion will ease my desire.
But this bread breaking feeds the fire.
I've no apology; no pardoning my game,
When push comes to shove, victory to shame.

One Ounce

In the last nine months I have lived in four different places. Not just stayed for a hot minute but so convinced of my permanent residency at each place that I sent that postcard to the Post Office every time to have my address changed. My intention at every place was to start over. Be good. Do well. I drank myself out of every single place with some intermittent spurts of couch surfing. And each time my possessions got fewer and fewer. I started out with a truckload and by the time I wound up at the last place I had everything in one pillowcase. The poverty line was beginning to look luxurious compared to the desolateness I lived under. I couldn't fathom financial comfort, never mind wealth.

Wealthy people were a constant supply of resentment. I looked at them and wondered if they knew any kind of sacrifice? Any kind of want? On really bad days I hated them. Thinking about them made me cry. I had packing tape holding my work shoes together and they were complaining about the valet parking at the new French restaurant. I felt a huge sense of entitlement against people whose wallets were not echoing bare. I imagined what I would do with one of their paychecks. I had all these big plans of paying off these medical debts and even bigger plans of paying off this ridiculous tuition debt. That's the one I hated the most. I spent six years and nearly $22,000 in loans dying for a degree. Now that I had one I was still serving coffee to a bunch of ass wipes and rubbing pennies together hoping they would magically procreate into a nickel.

On more rational days I would remind myself that despite my extremely modest income a huge part of my financial prison was due to the fact that I was a raging alcoholic and drug addict. It is not cheap to support a habit that requires constant attention and action. But this rational thought only made me more depressed that this *was* who I was and I would most certainly have to drink this depression away, thus continuing the cycle that perpetually landed me in the ER and consequently drained my bank account. To those who are unsure, an ambulance is by far the most expensive mode of transportation available. I looked at one bill that showed the mileage driven was 2.1 miles and I was charged $600. I wasn't even awake for it. Damn. Did someone give me a Swedish massage during those 2.1 miles? Was I served champagne and caviar through the intravenous drip? Was the Queen of England driving that damn ambulance?

I've spent the better part of the past two years drinking myself to sleep. Without alcohol I couldn't sleep. I tried on several occasions, okay or maybe twice, to just go to bed like normal people do. It was miserable. My body had gotten so used to the alcohol routine that it didn't seem to remember how to function without it. This wasn't necessarily alarming to me though. What was, was the fact that the ABC store closed at 9pm and that would mean chugging beer which was so filling and laborious. But I did what I needed to do.

It all boils down to one ounce. If I have that first one it is inevitable that a thousand will follow. If I never take that first one then nothing happens. For all the fucking annoying little sayings in AA this is one that I actually don't mind remembering...one drink is too many and a thousand is never enough. Drinking for me has been a devastating and highly successful career. It has given me personality, humor, courage, generosity, and adventure. On the other hand, it has taken every last remnant of life from me. The success of drinking always happens all at once. Like, blah blah blah, few shots, few beers, and BAM. I'm smart, attractive, clever, and wildly creative.

But the destruction has never been so swift. It comes deceptively, and quietly. Subtle of course but deep. There is nothing superficial about the damage. It seeps deep into my body all the way to the molecules of my soul. Oozing so methodically that it seems to have its own life. Its own course and plan. Then many years later I look in the mirror and am horrified. This face is repulsive to me. Those eyes are lying constantly and begging pathetically. I go from the cusp of utopia to the digger of my own grave in what feels like an instant and an eternity. I hate this more than I have hated anything else yet it is the one thing I cannot bring myself to imagine denying. Hit me. Hit me. Hit me again, I really hate it. One more time. Hit me. I have this terrible suspicion that I will continue to believe I'm drawing new water from this old well time and again if something doesn't happen. A feeling that since this is the perpetual flow of my life, nothing will stop the normal momentum I'm spinning in.

I've been asking for a miracle for years. Most times the asking comes from the tiles of a bathroom floor. Bleeding and crying and throwing up everything I worked so hard to get down. I am an amazing prayer maker when I'm drunk. I am most sincere. Most desperate. Most near something bigger than myself. Then I'll wake up some hours later and curse myself both for praying when I was drunk and for believing it would work. I hate myself the most when I'm hung-over. Feeling so sick and drained and exhausted. My mind operates on some sort of Neanderthal back-up system while I wait for the more conventional part of me to kick in. I am so thirsty and craving the grotesqueness of greasy fast food. I want a scalding shower and a cool, clean bed. Normally though after nights like these I have to settle for a few cigarettes and deodorant before I hurry into work.

This isn't what I signed up for asshole. I thought we'd have a few and enjoy ourselves like I'd seen hundreds of times before. I thought we'd sip slowly and romantically and look sophisticated and classy. Look like adults. I thought we'd spend a few hours poring over pointless, strangely articulate conversation that would otherwise never have surfaced. I thought we'd wake up the next morning feeling fine, maybe a little hungry and then have a cup of black coffee and go on with the rest of our fine Saturday morning. I thought we'd do this occasionally and have cocktails with cute names and petite umbrellas swimming in the tops of our glasses. I thought this would be harmless. Uneventful. Nothing noteworthy, never mind worth writing about. But now, like most catastrophes, retrospect is a most unenviable position to be in. Years into this I now see the truth of it all. Maybe on some days I just see part of the truth but even a fraction of the truth is so painful. It's why you are sold with denial, it makes the truth look much less real. Even as I write I know I will close the laptop when I'm done and walk over to this hole in the wall bar and stew over you. I consume you almost effortlessly and this pleases you. You'll wait until I think I'm warm and in control and normal then you'll pound me with the most wretched taste of shame. It's the same shame every time but it feels more and more oppressive with each sip. Then I think I will wash you away with more of you. More of you. More of you.

The Witch

One of my best friends is a pastor's wife, but before she was this, we were in college in the mountains and coming up with awesome ideas together. We would spend hours reading and writing and pretending to study on the largest purple couch you have ever laid eyes on. We were so easily amused then and found contentment in such simple things. For example, we invented a game called Hall Tennis that was basically a combination of soccer and tennis and as you suspected, it was played in the hall. We played this game during finals until the psycho downstairs tattled on us for making too much racket and our gaming was shut down. We also tried to write a story together one time without talking and she was the left hand on the keyboard and I was the right hand. It was going great until I couldn't stop accidentally typing the letter "T" and she almost killed me. We would laugh so hard and we ate what we wanted and we went where we wanted and we knew only enough to make life seem really fucking amazing. This all seems so long ago now that my four best friends are all married with little babies and there aren't enough hours in the day or money in the bank to spoil ourselves with being foolish.

Now, let me tell you a little tale about one great idea she came up with all on her own. We were taking an Intro to Journalism class together (by the way she was a terrible classmate...one time the professor took us outside to scold us because we kept talking and giggling and when we returned to our seats I was suffering a near panic attack of humiliation but she put her headphones back on and very loudly said how funny that was, needless to say I died twice). Anyway, we had to write a Halloween article because it was October. I found the assignment only emphasized our professor's utter lack of creativity but also was so dull and overdone that I wanted to interview a bag of candy and call it a day.

My friend, on the other hand, believed we could basically reinvent the wheel and come up with a new and exciting Halloween topic. She decided we should interview a witch. I kindly told her that witches aren't real (she was very naïve; I helped her a lot) but she insisted they are, so she asked the professor if we could secure this topic before any other genius in the class beat us to it. He agreed to our idea and then told us there was a "witch" living at the bottom of the mountain in a town about 45 minutes away. This is how Kalle is though. She comes up with an idea and it magically happens. If anyone else had decided to do this, if a witch asked to interview a witch, the professor would have laughed at her stupid idea. But Kalle had ideas that were nearly reality before the whole thought had formed. This is also how Kalle is, when she says something, I always agree. I have agreed to many, many bizarre and strange things because I have trusted her without question. In all the years I have known her, this particular event was the only one where I maybe should have hesitated a little bit. Or at least put up a fight or something. But I figured it would be a really fun car trip and I'd get to say "told you so" and then we'd go home and write a story about how witches don't actually exist but we hunted for one anyway.

As it turned out though, witches are real and I really almost shit my pants that night. We drove down the mountain, got really lost, got locked in a bathroom stall, Kalle's back hurt and we had no cell phone reception. All of these pitfalls could have been sheer coincidence, but in hindsight I'm pretty sure we were doomed from the start. When we did finally arrive we both realized that neither of us actually called this woman to ask if we could stop by for a brief chat. We were novice journalists, rookie mistake.

I stood on her porch holding a clipboard and Kalle was holding a recorder and we bravely knocked on the door. An older woman with a big blonde curly wig opened the door. She did not greet us or address us, she just stared at us briefly and walked back into her house from the open door. We took that to mean we were warmly invited in. To this day I have never met anyone whose eyes did what that woman's eyes did. The Witch had some other guests over, so we sat at her table and waited while they finished talking. As I was waiting I noticed the lovely furnishings in her small home. Namely, the wood coffin serving as the coffee table and the human skull sitting on top of it. I could see into her bedroom from where I sat and I could see many other wigs draped over the bedpost. There were white oleander flowers and green candles everywhere.

Suddenly, this feeble old woman began to look and *feel* unfamiliar and shifty. It felt very crowded and unsafe. In a short time, it was our "turn." I fell into some sort of "scared-shitless" trance and remained mute and unblinking through most of our "interview." Kalle, undaunted, plowed on with the most rigorous and award-winning interview I'd ever been a part of. The Witch seemed particularly drawn to Kalle and I feel certain it was because she wore Jesus-like clothing. The Witch was either aware of this and felt intimidated or ignored me because I was so completely useless that I was rendered a non-threat.

We/Kalle asked the usual questions you would want to ask a witch. Where's your broom? Do you have a wart on your nose? Are you a good witch or a bad witch? And when we got to the, "Can you read minds?" she aptly demonstrated this by spouting off several life events of mine. It wasn't exactly "mind-reading" because I wasn't thinking those things, but she clearly knew me. She knew things that Kalle didn't, and when I did begin to think, "Please shut up, shut up, shut up," she did just that. Mid-sentence, she stopped. She claimed to be able to predict the future too and even after Kalle adamantly told her not to, she went on to report things about Kalle's future. Odd things, and things that I'm happy to report have not come to pass. She knew about our lives at school on the mountain. She told us about several other strange abilities and tales from her living crypt.

And then she dropped the bomb. She told us she was a Christian and used the bible to do her spells and what not. At the time, I could not have cared less if she told me Jesus was in her kitchen fixing poison tea for all of us. I was not spiritual and did not care to be. Her claiming to be Christian was paramount to me claiming to have two feet...big deal witchy witch. But for Kalle, these were fighting words. And I saw the rage flash over Kalle's face when the Witch said this. I thought this was no time to be saving souls and maybe we should just let this one off the revival wagon. Kalle was angry that she would claim to be doing any of this in Christ and the angrier she got, the more amused the Witch became.

This was when her eyes became frightening. When she felt like she had the upper hand. Like she had us cornered and confused and she'd claim anything at that point to keep us off balance. She knew several scriptures and in my delirium, I have to admit that I was impressed. As I inwardly nodded my approval of her biblical knowledge, Kalle told her that even the Devil can quote scripture. I thought this was when she would hack our heads off with a rusty ax and hide our bodies in the pond out back with all the other curious, nosy journalists from the top of the mountain. I hated journalism. I hated Halloween. I hated bible-quoters. I hated that I was going to die in this witch's brew and the last thing I would see would be her creepy blue eyes and I would hear her cackling over the bible. She would probably drink my blood. Cut my hair off and make a wig. Oh my God, who did she kill to make all those wigs?

Clearly, she did not kill us, but she did scare the pants off me. I think Kalle was scared, but for different reasons. She was scared because this woman *was* powerful, she did have something unworldly about her and it was not of Christ and it was not of goodness. It was very real and it was invasive and haunting. Sort of like a bully from the underworld.

It is important to note that during our three-hour interview we did accomplish a few other noteworthy things. First of all, and I tell no lies, at one point the Witch had Kalle pinned on her back on the floor in a wrestling hold to prove to us that she used to be a professional wrestler. Second, she explained that the coffin was actually hers for when she had her own funeral. She put herself in a trance and held her own funeral. Hundreds of people attended, it made the front page of several newspapers and I crapped my pants for the tenth time that night when she showed us the papers. Third, she invited us to come back the following night (which was literally Halloween). She was going to have a séance and hotdogs. Which makes perfect sense. As we left and got into the car, she waved goodbye to us from her porch and said that she loved us. I yelled back to her that I loved her too. In the beautiful safety of Kalle's car, she asked me in disbelief why I told her I loved her. At that point I would have said anything to the woman, it just felt necessary to tell her I loved her. Going home we did not get lost, we had cell phone reception, and when we called our friends hysterically trying to recount everything, they thought we were joking and hung up on us. When we get home, they saw our faces and believed us immediately.

Our little assignment got us an "A" and was actually published on the front page of the paper in the little town at the bottom of the mountain. I picture the Witch reading the article and laughing with pride as she recalls how she scared us, her cackle echoing over the pond of dead journalists as she sticks pins in voodoo dolls that bear a striking resemblance to the two idiot college students at the top of the mountain.

Like I said at the beginning, Kalle is a pastor's wife now and we don't go witch hunting anymore. We are far too civilized for that. Now she spends her time raising children and a church and I spend my time writing about her one bad idea. I like to randomly drop in this tid-bit during conversations with her church people. "Yes, yes, lovely sermon, amen sister. Did you know Kalle took me to see a witch in college?" The intro line changes a bit from time to time and becomes slightly exaggerated, but it always has the same effect and I love it.

The glance at Kalle with a look that says, "Have I been lied to? Who are you and what is your real name?"

I think about the Witch from time to time and if she is still alive. She was old when we met her, so I wonder how she is doing now. Does she still light her green candles to let the spirits in? Does she still talk to the dead relatives of the townspeople? Does she wait around all year for overzealous college kids to find their way to her door? She was an old lady creep that I'm pretty sure wanted to offer me as a sacrifice, but instead, many years later, I find myself amused by our adventure and steadfast in my belief that supernatural things do exist. Things like Jesus, God, miracles, witches, and unicorns. Just kidding about the unicorn part, unless the Witch has one as a pet and in that case, I believe in unicorns.

Two Loves

Love 1

When we met? Oh, how I remember that moment. Not just a memory of the day or season, but the precise moment we came smashing into one another. He was charming and what's more, he was inviting and warm. So familiar and comfortable after only a subtle glance. I've never been a romantic, never even had a relationship prior to him...but in one split second he made me a weak-kneed, butterflies in the stomach type of teenage lover. He wooed and I came longingly as though we were long-lost lovers separated by ocean and age. He called to me with a tenderness I'd not experienced before. I laid down my apprehension and nerves with the ease one leaves their muddy shoes at the front door. To shake off the heaviness of his absence; to leave it at the door where all other misgivings were shut out. I was a girl on fire and he was equally enamored with the spark and sway of the inevitable "us." I was 13 and a bounty lay before me now that this door had been opened.

Three years in and his voice carries further and lingers longer than anyone else. My mother disapproves because he is rowdy and unpredictable. My friends are uncertain because he is not like the other boys. He seems much older, and much more grown than the other boys. Even more grown than us. But I am not offended by their up-turned noses. He came for me, found me, and even after three years I feel that he still pursues me as though this were a very long courtship. He is perseverant and steadfast in his affection for me. We sneak away when we can. The mystery of him and then of myself with him is intoxicating. Who am I with him and without him are so staggeringly different that I feel drawn to the riddle all the more. A pull and drag from his sheer presence. His scent. His confidence. His unflinching desire to get me.

I am 18 and the rush of him has aged me. His pace is breakneck and I trip over myself to keep up. I sense some cracks in our relationship, where he plows on and I stagger around unsure of the direction. But where I am weakest, he is most strong and carries me on through the indecision of it all. I go along with it, he hasn't been wrong yet. He hasn't betrayed or abandoned me. He hasn't lied or misguided. He has been the most reliable love and I scold myself for considering any alternative. The others are wary. They back away slowly and keep quiet about everything, including him. He is too much for them and I chalk it up to "misunderstanding."

I think I am in my early 20s. He must be ageless, but is handsome as ever. I have decided, without telling him, that we may not be compatible because I am exhausted and so lost. We are divorced in my mind but in reality he renews our vows every evening with gusto and vigor. The more weary I become the more empowered he seems to become. We are an oxymoron and I distract myself by thinking of the good times. Thinking about the first date in my childhood home. About our long and wonderful courtship. Our volatile but passionate relationship. I think about my patience and silence. His faithfulness and strong will to have it his way. I have decided to leave. I will leave him a note.

I have left many times, only to return to him. He remains faithful to me, but has become violent and cruel. I feel that he is punishing me for not returning his unashamed love of me. I have withheld from him. Ever so slightly, I have withheld from him and he will hunt me down for every last bit. He no longer needs just my time and affection. He needs everything and I handed over nearly all of it until I was left just one thing. But he wanted that one thing. Perhaps he wanted that one thing more than he wanted all the other things.

I am nearly 30 and I have seen my grave dug and re-dug a dozen times. He stands by with a shovel, always at the ready to throw me in. He has snatched all good things but one, and I unknowingly have clutched it just out of his reach. He mocks me and laughs at me for holding onto anything. He is unsatisfied with me while simultaneously promising me that we can get back to how it used to be. How it was on our first date when I looked lovingly at him and he spoiled me. I am so tired that I would likely agree to anything. I have straddled between "all or nothing" for so many years. I am going to leave and cash in my last thing.

Love 2

I saw her and loved her long before she noticed me. She didn't know I existed, but I knew all of her nuances. I knew the ins and outs of her before she knew them herself, but in exchange for my affection she gave me nothing but a passing glance.

The type of glance you would give a stranger. A beggar. A nuisance. But I am an undaunted suitor. A hapless romantic. I may be the underdog, the uninvited and intrusive, but I will inevitably be the one to bail her out. She'll eventually come to me and it doesn't even matter that when she finally notices me it will be out of fear and desperation. I won't shrink away. I won't betray what she doesn't even know I promised her. I won't abandon her even though she doesn't know we're together. I will lay waste to her misgivings and I will forget all the times she denied me. My sway will seem imperceptible to her, but it will be enough to move her. My love of her has no age, no time frame, no boundary. I can wait at the threshold longer than she can.

Don't get me wrong, her years are hard to bear as I watch. She is counting days and I am unfamiliar with that burden. To me, she is always a breath away. To her, I seem less and less feasible. Her friends are counting too. They know I'm pursuing, but the path is full of ugliness. She looks around suspiciously when she is alone, as if she is about to reluctantly invite me over. This stirs my hope. She seems wildly afraid of me; it is because she knows that I was right and she is unsure how to admit this. I'm not angry, just sad. It is nearly all sadness when your beloved turns away. But despite this, she senses me I know.

She is nearly grown and the space between us grows larger and larger. It has become apparent that she's met someone else and this really dampens the altar. She has no idea that he does not love her, that no one, in fact, loves her the way that I am capable of loving her. My anger is awakened, but not with her. It is an anger over things lost and unloved or poorly loved in spite of what I've promised. It is an anger over who she has invited in and who she has shut out. I look more and more like a beggar on her doorstep instead of the love she has been digging around for. Digging in wells with shallow waters and digging in hallowed land. She will notice me only in anger and will curse all the unlovely things because she has not let me in to love her well. She will misunderstand nearly everything.

Everyone has called me a madman for not letting this go. For not relenting. For not walking away when I've had every good reason to walk away. I am bound up and tied to a sinking ship, they say. But I know more and I know better and I can nearly laugh at the scoffing. For all that I have sacrificed, it would be unfair to me and to her to cave and give up now. The pursuit was not meant to be easy. She's had other relationships that have been challenging, so I know she can handle this one. Giving up would be equivalent to pretending I never decided to love her in the first place. And this is just not true. I cannot leave.

She continues to be suspicious and skeptical of me, although there are warm spots in her that cave a little when she is alone. The spots that her partner has worn very thin; those spots have become so human again because they are so tender. For as much as he has controlled her, he has accidentally made her more susceptible to hearing me. If he knew this, he would be so angry to have helped me at all. The more he ruins her, the more he readies her for me.

I have made preparations for her wedding and for her funeral. Both are as likely. A wedding with me or a funeral with him. The world looks at her with resentment and frustration because the choice looks so obvious. But to her, the good and the bad are inextricable at times. She has been deceived. She has deceived herself. She has married up to all the things that I have wept over. She has questioned and doubted me when I've given her no reason to. We have spoken so infrequently that the sound of my voice still frightens her. Yet, she hears me and that is enough. I am her last resort, her last hope. I am the last thing, and that is plenty for me.

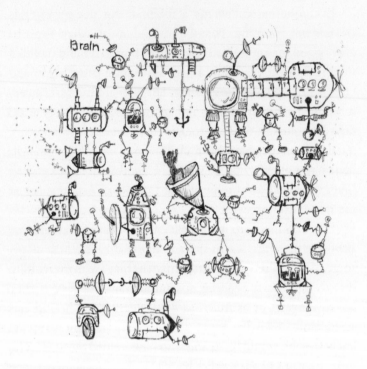

I HAVE STRUGGLED BETWEEN THESE two loves for most of my life. The first is my addiction that seemed to engulf and swallow me whole. I willing and unwillingly succumbed to its power for many years. There was a long time that I was enamored with it and believed it was to my benefit. I believed it not only helped and loved me, but that it was necessary. It quieted the loud and wrongly wired brain that misfired at the most inconvenient times. It soothed and comforted in a way that I could not do for myself and other people did not come close to doing for me. In solace and in gladness, this was the love I sought first and hardest. I forfeited almost everything to my addiction and I paid dearly for that delusional love. The love of an abusive spouse, to whom I repeatedly went back to in order to right the wrongs we had committed together.

The second love has been God. I have participated very little in this relationship. I have left all the heavy lifting and faithfulness to God. He has taken up that commitment every time without regret or question. I have spent a lot of time being angry with Him, blaming Him and then reluctantly going back to Him. I am reminded that Jonah spent most of his life being angry with God because he *knew* God's character so well. This comforts me because in my confusion and being unwell in my anger, I remember that it is because God refuses to give up and refuses to judge my sin that He is merciful to me, to my idols, and to everyone else who I give up on and judge. I am angry because I know the character of God well enough to know that I will not get what I deserve and that makes me feel guilty. I know that others will not get what they deserve and that makes me bitter. God cared for me long before I knew I needed care and then long after I was beyond the care of others.

I'm sure that what has felt miraculous in my life may only look like lucky turns of events to others. But it matters none to me because the nosy, invasive, and patient god that followed me around like a younger sibling tugging on my shirt has sustained me despite myself. To spend even one day sober and in my right mind is beyond what I might have prayed for when I laid at the mouth of death and insanity. It is a small token. One day. But it is one more day I didn't see coming.

Cube Farm

My boss comes over this morning about an hour into the day. Dear God, why are you over here?

"Did you guys notice anything different today?" He is more than mildly excited. The last time my boss wanted us to guess a super special surprise, I was secretly hoping he was about to tell us the company went bankrupt and we were all going to be laid off. We play along like good lemmings and look around our cubes.

"The chairs were steam-cleaned last night!" He cannot stand the suspense anymore and divulges the big news. I am at odds with myself about how I should react. Do I stare blankly at him in calloused disgust for his unyielding love of all things corporate? Or do I continue to play along and stand up enthusiastically to examine my steamy clean, badass chair? I play along. It's easier to play along. I want to buy my boss a bumper sticker that says, "I ♥ My Cubicle" and then buy myself one that says, "I Fucking Torched My Cubicle."

The lady at the front desk is sort of an enigma in the office. She is in her late 50s, maybe early 60s, and is supposed to be answering the phones and occasionally stuffing envelopes. What she really does is talk on the phone to her other receptionist friends around Charlotte about their academically gifted and charming grandchildren. When this cesspool of excitement dries up, she moves on to discussing the latest celebrity makeovers. She has tomes of People magazines and catalogs from every department store ever established. I didn't know the catalog business was still a viable one until I saw this woman.

The enigma part is that she is paid to sit up there and piddle around all day. I found out she is a breast cancer survivor and the boss is too afraid to replace her because of this cancer thing. Could you really live with yourself if you fired someone who had already beaten cancer? There is a special place in hell for this sort of work place happening. Apparently even CEOs can be cornered into behaving civilly if faced with threats of eternal damnation or old ladies with super durable, cancer-resistant boobs. I kid, this is probably not the case at all, but we all sort of give her a free pass to free load because she is older than all of us and she yells inspiring things like, "Cancer didn't beat me and neither will your silly rules about working."

I completely envy her and even respect her when I am not consumed with bitterness about receiving verbal warnings for moving the water cooler to an inconvenient location. She bucks the system. She reads her magazines and chats it up on the company dime/receptionist salary. The rest of us shuffle around nervously, knowing full well we are all cogs in a wheel and scared to death to turn the corner and run into the CEO or, worse yet, the Human Resources Manager.

The Human Resources Manager. Remember that special place in hell where they send cruel CEOs? That section is organized and run efficiently under the say-so of Human Resource Managers. Had this woman been around during WWII, I honestly believe we would have seen different results. The fear of God could easily be confused for the fear of Ms. Azburk. For example, last Friday Ms. Azburk was standing at my co-worker's desk. My co-worker, Helen, is president of the Booster Club (the existence of a Booster Club in an all adult environment is akin to putting tax returns and mortgage statements in a kindergarten class). Helen and Ms. Azburk are going over a big list and organizing piles of stuff. For the sake of appearing interested and friendly, I ask the ladies, "What's all this stuff?"

"It's for the company picnic tomorrow, you're coming right?" Ms. Azburk asks/demands. Oh no. Oh why did I even ask? Why would I even open my mouth for such drivel? I am not going to the picnic and I am preparing to confess this.

"Oh that's right, the picnic. Well I won't be able to attend, but I hope you have fun," I say with feigned disappointment and an exaggerated frowny face to solidify the utter loss I'm surely feeling. The next 30 seconds happen in slow motion. Ms. Azburk stands up. Stands up very slowly, unfolds herself like a beast, like a demigod. Her eyes narrow into beads – little red beads burning into my mortal skull. I have sinned against corporate America. I have blasphemed.

"You're not coming? Why wouldn't you come? You know the company is *paying* for you." Her words are slow and deliberate and I feel six years old. In a split second I have half a mind to tell her my reasons for not attending: (1) I am not being paid to go and therefore will not participate at work for free. (2) There are few things I can think of that would be less enjoyable than a Saturday afternoon with my workmates, namely death. (3) I already had plans to take a shower on Saturday and I cannot reschedule that. The rest of her conversation was more of the same, mainly her siphoning my soul with her glares and then dismissing me back to joining the scores of other peons.

I go back to my desk and read a story online about a flight attendant who lost his marbles at work. The passengers were being rude and acting like fools and he simply had enough. After the plane has landed, this brave and probably very handsome man announces that he quits, and before pulling the cord to inflate the emergency escape slide he grabs a six pack of beer. He slides down the world's largest bounce house with his beer and walks off the job.

I lean back in my very clean chair and marvel at his display of utter brilliance. I overlook the fact that he was later arrested for breaking two million federal aviation laws, one of which was stealing beer that cost the airline $112 because for some reason going high up in the sky makes beer very expensive. I also overlook the fact that he'll probably have a really hard time finding another job. I let myself live vicariously through him. Through the savior of all minions working for the "man." I want to write him a letter of encouragement, but I'm not sure how to send mail to a penitentiary. I want to tell him that his momentary break with reality was not only rational and courageous, but also heroic. I want to mail him a medal or trophy or food stamps or something. I want to tell him that he's not missing much in corporate America, except for the clean upholstery and alcohol-free picnics. I'd also tell him that I fantasize about copying him at my office. I'd have to change a few things up, but it'd go like this: I'd hang up on my boss, throw my chair down the stairs, take the entire water cooler off the stand and then take the elevator down that is meant for clients only. I would strut all the way outside, salute the building and then run like hell because I don't want to go to jail.

Ghost Writer

In class this week with a small group of freshmen, I had us all poised and ready to begin a new unit. The first lesson was complex and required that I read to them some directions before we went to school on that dumb book. I had the lights off, like I always do, and began to read. I always have the lights off for two reasons. One, I can see and *hear* the lights, so my head feels like it is going to bleed out my ears if I have to listen to the lights one more minute. Second, for some reason when I turn off the lights the small demon-possessed teenagers that were once foaming at the mouth calmly and sweetly take their seats in what can only be described as an act of God and Congress.

So in our silent, dark, post-lunch classroom I began to read. According to my watch, I read for approximately three minutes. According to the student watch, I began reading directions on a Tuesday and wrapped up around Saturday. After I read, I noticed that one of the kids had her head down on the desk, sleeping soundly. I tapped her head and told her we were about to begin. She perked up in her chair, yawned, stretched and said, "Oh, I'm sorry Ms. Regan, your story was just so boring." I thought about explaining in even more boring detail that I wasn't telling a story, I was giving instructions. Instructions about learning and doing well and without them she'd probably fail the ninth grade, which in turn would mean she would probably die an old bitter widow, drunk and smoking cheap cigarettes and crying about how she wished she listened to her boring teachers. And because this is a public school I can't even go into the awful fate of smoking cheap cigarettes.

But instead I accidentally laughed out loud because it was funny. Without the burden of a filter, this girl just told me exactly how boring I was and she wasn't even rude or mean about it. She just told me the truth like she was telling me the room was dark. Maybe to me, what I was reading were ill-conceived, dry instructions; but to the girl, it was a really terrible, boring story. But it *was* a story. This is how writing can be. You'll put pen to paper a thousand times and most people will fall asleep to the droning of your words. You'll labor over a thesaurus and make lists and lists about things that should be written. A single sentence will mock you as you try to go to bed that night. You'll daydream about the cover and title page of your book, even though not a single page has been written. Then, one day you'll be minding your own business not thinking about writing at all and accidentally tell someone a story. A story that never crossed your mind because on a horribly ordinary Wednesday nothing seems organic or good. But that story will sneak up and bite you in the ass. Most of the stories we tell are never written down. Never even acknowledged as stories, never re-told in all the glory of a "tell it again!" occasion. Most will be forgotten before we make it home to paper. Even worse, most of those stories will bore and slide away into the day as mere conversation, directions, requests, insults.

We are prolific storytellers. Sometimes our ramblings come out so hideous that the audience is wise to sleep through the epic fail. But sometimes, the story feels just right. Like the first cool day of autumn and you unbury the winter clothes. Shake out your favorite sweatshirt and within minutes it begins to graph into your skin. At any rate, the storytelling was never reserved exclusively for writers, it just so happens to be that writers take up the tedious task of recording the often boring happenings of planet Earth and her meandering humans.

When I decide to write one of three things happens. I either sit down briefly and then remember that I have about a dozen very important errands that should be accomplished first because I won't be able to focus on the writing if I am worrying about cat food and tire pressure and world peace. Or I go to sit down and realize about four hours later that I had never actually made it to the desk but somehow have been napping peacefully in my bed the whole time. It can be draining to write, so my body probably instinctively knew it needed to rest up and/or hibernate while the keyboard prepared itself for greatness. Or lastly, I sit down to write and almost like a ghost, something moves my lithe fingers across the keyboard like we are playing the piano. It typically lasts only 45 minutes to an hour and then the ghost goes to bed or to run errands, but while he is here, it is lovely.

The ghost can be very picky and inconvenient. Sometimes he likes the cold quiet of my room. Sometimes he lurches at me when I am driving, like in scary movies where the stupid, weak female is driving alone at night down a long winding road and everyone in the galaxy knows there is a murderer in the backseat except her. Then she looks in her rearview mirror because she heard something stirring back there and BAM he slices her head off with an ax. Okay, maybe not exactly like that, but he does like to get me while I'm driving and I have to contort my body to reach the napkin stuffed under my seat so that I can write down what he says. Then I find the scraps of his ideas littered all over my room, my car, my purse. The unwasted idea that miraculously made it to paper while I was driving down East Blvd. with my toes. If you think I am exaggerating here, let me convince you of my remarkable driving skills (save for the driving while intoxicated charge, minor detail). One time I was late for a wedding and had to shave my legs while driving there. On several occasions I changed entire outfits while driving. I went from business casual to college chic in a matter of four miles.

Anyway, sometimes the bits make no sense at all. For instance, "Put an 8 beside each eyeball," apparently made sense to the ghost but now that I'm looking at it many months later I have no idea what the hell he was talking about, but I save the scrap because it was sacred at some point and maybe when I'm old and dying this will mean something very lovely to me. Sometimes the ghost believes it is most helpful if he simply lists things prior to delivering his good news. I recently sat down to finish an essay about Christmas and I got to number 11 before I realized I was making a list of "Phenomenal Pairs."

1. Latte & Cigarette

2. NPR Weekend Shows & Driving

3. Candy & Coffee

4. Pancakes & Milk

5. Clean Sheets & Open Windows (in bedroom)

6. Sunday-night Football & Three-day Weekend

7. Chinese Takeout & Scary Movie

8. College Rule Notebook & Ultra-fine, Gel-roller, Black Pen

9. "Christmas Vacation" & Christmas Eve

10. Newspaper & Patio

11. Car Wash & Full Tank of Gas

Then I couldn't remember what I was supposed to be writing and decided that Karma or Jesus probably wanted this list for something really important. So I did what comes naturally, the ghost and I took a smoke break. During the "break" I realized what a bitter winter it had been in North Carolina and after standing in the cold, I needed a warm shower to bring blood flow back to my extremities. I stood in the hot shower for 30 minutes thinking about how I would type without fingers. Then I thought about which limb I could lose that would have the least effect on my quality of life. Which naturally led to me remembering when I was a kid and I prayed that God would make me deaf because I thought the external noise lessening would help with the internal noise. I was fairly certain He would do this deaf-making thing so I taught myself sign language to be ahead of the game. I never lost my hearing, but I still know sign language.

After the shower it was time for a snack. The snack called for another cigarette and so the vicious cycle of writing continues ad nauseam.

Three days later the ghost and I returned to my computer. The battery had died and this situation delayed us another hour or so because when I went to find the power cord I realized that I should brew coffee and fix a snack before going back upstairs. I got the cream from the fridge and was immediately annoyed when I realized it was a new carton. Who puts these stupid little plastic tabs in the openings of new cartons? They are a pain to get off and now, not only would I have to go to the fridge, but also the trashcan to throw away the little tab. I decided I didn't have time to go to the trashcan because I had a lot of important writing to do, so I only tore off the tab half way. It was open just enough to dribble out cream into my cup but not enough to fall off, which would require the second trip across the kitchen to the trashcan. I am so clever, I thought. I had beaten the man. The man that put this time-wasting tab in my cream carton. The same man who put batteries in three-inch thick plastic that can only be opened with a tree trimmer. The same man who put all that shrink wrapped plastic and, for the sake of overkill, the microscopic strip of sticky tape on new CDs. Oh what? No one buys CDs anymore? Well I buy them and I hate opening them, it takes away so much time from writing the next great American novel. Then I was struck by the ghost who told me we should be writing these things down. I ran upstairs, without my coffee, and began a new list.

I also count writing as a gift. Not as in a talent or skill, but a literal present given to me without the expectation of gratitude or returning the favor in kind. Most of the time I forget to be grateful that amongst all the really difficult

things, I have been given a profoundly useful escape route
through writing. When I am overwhelmed by what has not
been given to me, I am brought back to reality with the blank
and bountiful paper at my disposal. I also think that because
I was entrusted to write I had to be given good material.
Stage left, enter: Alcoholic. Curtain pull, fade lights, enter:
Questionable mental stability. Grand finale, cue orchestra,
enter: For good measure let's make things blow up and catch
on fire and stop breathing right in her way so she'll have to
write them down. Also, we should discreetly add several
unsavory and bat-shit crazy people along the way so that she
doesn't decide to become an accountant or something. And
that's a wrap, costume change, stage sequel.

Sheep

Winter in the South is a lot like a warm bath that cooled when someone rudely opened the bathroom door to ask if the trash had been taken to the curb. It isn't freezing or terrible, but it is just enough cool air to make it uncomfortable. Our tragic winters are why so many Northerners move down here. They are escaping the abominable snowman up near the Arctic Circle where they once lived. They come down here with their fur parkas and sleds and heated seats and mittens that plug into the auxiliary of their car radios. Amateurs. Their first winter is barely registering on their frost bitten biological thermometers.

The calendar changes to December and they brace themselves for the slap across the face that Mother Nature so often delivered with gusto up north. But down here, she is subdued, almost languid like she had a cocktail around the Mason Dixon line and all the evil conspiracies she whipped up for the winter slowly fade away. The further down she goes, the deeper her stupor and she is less and less likely to act like the mother fucker she pretends to be when she is up near the top of the globe. Then about every 20 years she decides the South is giving her a bad reputation and she needs to up her game to reestablish her dominance. She is greedy for gossip about her and she begs to be the bitch of winter we all thought we'd escaped when we settled into the warm hammock of the South.

That is exactly what happened this year. That old broad sobered up and smashed our forgetfulness of winter. Some massive storm froze half the country for a few days, including the South. A friend of mine from the North was personally offended. She had just moved here for the sole purpose of avoiding bitter winters. She had barely sent back the U-haul when the polar blast froze her ass to her new home. She had droves of good things to say about us and her new home until the seven-degree weather jumped up out of nowhere and then she only had sour looks for all of us, as though her new neighbors had orchestrated this to scare her back. I watched the news to see how cold other parts of the country were and marveled at the severity of earth and how hormonal and moody she seemed these past few days. It was colder in Atlanta than it was in Moscow. Colder in Chicago than it was in the Arctic and colder in Michigan than it was on Mars. Then two weeks after this cold snap, we got a freak snowstorm.

When you live in the South this is how you prepare for a snowstorm: the radio says we are expected to get one inch of snow and the storm is currently just west of Tennessee and moving our direction in the next 24 hours or so. You should panic, you are already too late. Total chaos as you get in your car wearing every article of clothing you own because God forbid you get stuck out there and are stranded in your car for days. You go to the store where every other resident is buying milk, bread, and eggs. Maybe we are all going to make bread pudding or maybe we are all going to freeze and die, but either way, at least we all made it to the grocery store.

Then while driving home you notice the road crews have put salt on the roads. But the salt shimmers in the sun (it's still 55 degrees and sunny) and you're unsure if it's actually salt or maybe its ice. Maybe while you were in the store it started to hail and sleet; maybe while you were in the store pigs took flight and I shit roses. You slow down and put your hazards on like the other drivers. We are bad drivers in any weather, but we are always courteous and eager to warn others of the eminent, deadly inch of snow coming to kill us. You can smell the snow in the air, and it's not just you that can smell it. The City Officials can smell it too and they cancel school and mandate a city-wide curfew to ensure everyone's safety. That's right, I said they canceled school. Can you blame them? We are ill-equipped to deal with this type of weather so instead of carry on, we simply hunker down and through the weeping and gnashing of teeth we may or may not see a snowflake. But the threat is there. Looming over us like we lost a bet and now owe too much money to a hustler we can't hide from.

Then it begins. A single solitary snowflake about the size of a really big molecule falls from the sky. Our panic gives way to marvel. The chaos of preparing to be a survivor in a post-apocalyptic North Carolina gives way to the really sweet beauty of something so quiet and soft. I imagine it is like God dropping sheep from the sky. Everything goes quietly into the night and we lay around praying it won't melt so we can see it again in the morning.

The Northerners think we are idiots and over-reacting. They laugh at our poor handling of snow because to them it is a daily occurrence. Some of us down here heaped some of the snow into a Ziploc bag and put it in the freezer as a souvenir from the night God dropped sheep on us. The Northerners can't imagine why anyone would want any sort of keepsake from this. They curse it and shovel it and nothing closes because of it. They are not afraid of it like we are. They are annoyed with it because it is nothing more than an inconvenience. We panic because we are unfamiliar with it and then we run around outside screeching and licking it because it is so beautiful. Have you ever thought about this? Being so overcome by the beauty of something that you go out there and literally try to taste it. Like your eyes and ears and hands are not enough to get it. You need to taste it too!

Then I start thinking about two things. Number 1: It's all fun and games making fun of us until a hurricane blows through the North of the country and they're all freaking out and whole states are being washed out to sea like they're going to rejoin the mother land. And in the South, when there is a hurricane, we sit outside in bathing suits, drinking beer and taunting the storm to give us her best shot. Number 2: This rift in reaction is so much like how it feels to run into God. Instead of telling you more about how we can turn into really psycho rednecks while waiting for a hurricane, I'm going to tell you about number 2.

Sometimes God chases after me and I'm like, "Oh you again? You're a pain in the ass. Go away and leave me alone. I'm telling you this isn't worth it." Because I don't want to be interrupted or convicted to change, and I definitely don't want my plans to be postponed because I've put together something really awesome. I'm sitting in my own throne and feasting with a whole host of idols that wouldn't see kindly to me inviting Jesus. We are slap drunk on everything from sadness to boredom. We're getting high off of everything and nothing and the irritating thought of God wanting His seat back seems petty and as dumb as those plug-in mittens the Northerners bring from their igloos down to our oasis. We poke holes in the theology of loving well and serving others. We marvel in our own invention and self-made worth. The same worth that will melt like the snow-sheep. Evaporate. Poof. Gone. Then we'll just start over. We'll make better excuses that can hold up to stronger arguments. We'll have better defenses against the wiser intruders. We'll lick our wounds and covet the feeling that we have created our own rapture. These fairy tales will hold more weight and more promise than God.

I've seen this perspective take hold in my own life and in the lives of those I love. Us humans make very poor lab subjects. God set it up to be good and then He started dropping us in. The experiment got off to a terrible start and has been going downhill ever since. We stack the odds against us ourselves. We chase after poison. We execute well-armed assaults against the people we once loved. We make losing bets without even seeing the game. We criticize and judge each other because it feels a little bit like success when we do. We shame each other into behaving how we think we ought to. We sit pious and righteous in our own thrones, leaving no room for anyone else in our crazed little kingdoms.

Then sometimes, running into God is more like tasting snow. I'll be sinking and groping for anything. Desperate as hell and crying like a psycho. God will come creeping in the back door and I'm like, "Where the hell have you been!? Please help me, help me dear God!" And even though He should just roll His eyes and step over my mess, instead, He'll hold my hair back while I'm heaving and gasping for breath. This kind of encounter feels so new and foreign. I am both afraid and relieved. Terrified and excited. I am right where panic ebbs into realizing it is all going to be okay. The fight or the issue or the elephant in the room still exists, but it is going to be subdued by a king.

In between these two places feels like it would be a little less manic. But humans don't do well in the middle of a god spectrum. We move continuously back and forth. Whiplashed by our own great upheavals. I think the best we can hope for is that when it's over, or as "over" as it's going to get, we can look back and see how pretty it was to see the sky full of something so strange and foreign. So bizarre that we had to taste it. Because we'll never have this perspective while we're zipping over the spectrum. Because we don't see the change happening while it's happening because it's too painful. While it's ugly, we gradually begin to resent the very people who have waited patiently because our own tragedy will ease for them in a week or so. We believe we suffer alone or suffer in some unique, new way. We don't know who is praying and even if we did know, we wouldn't believe it'd do any good anyway. We don't see all the other people in the same boat because they just look so much more composed than we do. Because we can't fathom the world ever looking any different than it does in that moment. We can't picture movement and momentum toward God. We can't imagine that half-full glass because it has been so damn long. Because mercy never has a flavor until we taste it.

Acknowledgments

I would like to thank my family and extended family of friends. I would also like to thank coffee and good folk music. Lastly, thank you to my aunts and uncles for being the best storytellers in the world.

About the Author

Tessie lives in Charlotte, NC, which has reportedly been named the best place on earth by several unofficial and anonymous sources. She has a real-person job that pays real-people bills, but more importantly she enjoys writing for the sake and love of words. She would like to be friends; email her at regantessie@yahoo.com.